The Alchemy of the Heart

The Alchemy of the Heart

Life's Refining Process to Free Us from Ourselves

Luci Swindoll

MULTNOMAH PRESS
PORTLAND, OREGON 97266

All quotations at the beginning of each chapter and the division of each part are taken from *Report to Greco*, by Nikos Kazantzakis (New York: Bantam Books, 1971).

Unless otherwise indicated, all scripture references in this volume are from The Living Bible, © 1971 by Tyndale House Publishers, Wheaton, Ill.

Cover design and illustration: Larry Ulmer

THE ALCHEMY OF THE HEART
© 1984 by Multnomah Press
Printed in the United States of America

Library of Congress Cataloging in Publication Data
Swindoll, Luci, 1932-
    The alchemy of the heart.

1. Swindoll, Luci, 1932-   2. Single women—
United States—Biography.   I. Title
HQ800.2.S94   1984   305.4'890652'0924   84-6984
ISBN 0-88070-052-1

    85 86 87 88 89 90 – 10 9 8 7 6 5 4 3 2

This book is dedicated to six friends:

Panagiotis and Maria
Sophia
Achilles and Klea
Madelene

A Greek family from Athens with powers of alchemy.

For fourteen years their acceptance and love
have enlarged the boundaries
of my home, my horizons, and my heart.

Contents

Foreword		9
Prologue—**THE CHEMISTRY**		11

PART I. THE METALS

Chapter

1.	My Grandparents	17
2.	My Father	29
3.	My Mother	43
4.	My Older Brother	55
5.	My Younger Brother	65
6.	My Friends	77
7.	My Mentors	89

PART II. THE FURNACE

Chapter

8.	School	107
9.	Opera	117
10.	Projects	129
11.	Work	139
12.	Solitude	149
13.	Church	159
14.	Travels	171

Epilogue—**THE GOLD**		181
Acknowledgements		185

Foreword

I pleaded with her not to do it, but she wouldn't be silenced. She had to let it all hang out . . . well, most of it anyway. After reading—and laughing my way through—the chapter on her older brother, I thought to myself that if my friends read that, I will be finished! Some will think I was the family clown! Luci attests to a memory that would win contests against elephants, and my own failure in that regard leaves me at a disadvantage to set her straight on the data. At least you have here her version of the family story.

Most of the last twenty-five years we have been separated by thousands of miles. Yet it seems that the distance has only served to draw us closer together in our appreciation for one another. I look back on the spats we had as children as utterly meaningless in view of the high esteem I've come to have for my only sister. It seems a shame we couldn't have enjoyed each other as much when we were youngsters.

I often wish she were closer (my wife and four children share this sentiment); perhaps because I've always felt she was so willing to listen, so ready to understand, so helpful in a thousand ways. Each of our children has come to love Aunt Luci because she has always been so attentive and full of life with them. But I have a very special place in my heart for her. For me she has been the perfect tonic (or alchemist?), the dearest friend, and the greatest encouragement on many occasions.

In so many ways Luci is unique, not at all like her two

brothers. Both Charles and I are contented husbands and fathers. Yet she has certainly managed to make her single life an abounding and exciting experience. Even if she reaches the century-mark, I cannot conceive of her ever being the typical "old maid." In other ways she is very much like her brothers. She loves people. She loves a challenge. She enjoys work. She appreciates integrity. She strives for excellence.

One thing she doesn't mention in the book is a matter that has enhanced my life for over thirty years. Surely it's the nicest thing she ever did for me. Following her first year in college she introduced me to a young lady who had just graduated from the same school. During Luci's freshman year Erma Jean Hensley had been a special friend, helping her adjust to the new environment. Ever since then she's been enriching my environment . . . as my wife. Where would I be without Luci?

Everyone who knows Luci knows she loves life. And in this book she tells us why. She also shows us how we can enjoy life more fully. As you read, listen to what she says about family, friends, music, projects, solitude, and walking with God. She's for real. No man has ever been able to completely captivate her free spirit—unless it was Daddy—but she has captivated a lot of us. Watch out . . . she may captivate you!

Orville Earl Swindoll

Prologue
THE CHEMISTRY

About ten years ago in the Lima, Peru, airport, I met a man from Chicago who had lost his passport. He was, shall we say, panic stricken. "What am I going to do?" he kept asking. "That one little document has all the valuable information on it that I need to get home. Without it, I'm stuck here with no credentials."

I remember looking at him, thinking, "Poor man. He'll probably be in Peru forever." Then I checked my purse to be sure my own passport was there for fear I could be in the same predicament. When I touched it, I held onto it for a few minutes as I realized it was probably at that moment the most valuable thing I owned.

It's a funny thing about documents of record. I used to think a birth certificate was so odd. Why do I need such a document? The very fact that I'm standing here proves I was born. Or a passport? If I'm in another country, somehow I got there. But documents of record give credence to more than just the obvious. They serve as the starting point for determining genuineness or value.

For instance, when we were born, our mothers wrote all our vital statistics in a baby book, in order to look at it, refer to it from time to time, show it to others, and to have a personal instrument of information which became the initial touchstone for our future physical development. School years brought the honorable or dishonorable report card—that official and all-encompassing piece of paper which acquainted our parents with a certain aspect of our growth not directly under their supervision, and which usually brought us good or ill. Receiving enough of these little cards with acceptable numbers or letters resulted in our attaining a diploma or a degree. Remember that first diary of yours in which you stored the most sacred and secret of all personal information? Do you recall your college thesis? Your marriage license? The grant deed to your land and property deed to your house? All documents of record.

And you're thinking, "Oh, yeah. I remember all those things, and I know precisely where they are. I stuck them in the upper right-hand drawer of that old desk which we sold to the Wilson family in 1973, who subsequently moved to the island of Sicily, where everything was lost in a volcanic eruption."

Documents have a way of being without significance or interest when we don't need them for reference, and much like the Holy Grail when they are the object of our search. (Such was the case of the man in the Lima airport.) Why are they so important? Because they distill all the essential facts from a particular period of our lives, and they give, as it were, written credence to that point of time. They enable us to have a true point of beginning as we consider how we've changed or how far we've come from that moment. There is something in each one of us that makes us want to measure development or record change—especially if it's positive. That's why we easily recall or diligently record our weight loss from Day One of Diet, the money we're accumulating in our savings account, the hours we've spent in working overtime, or the goals we've accomplished that began with a dream.

God, too, records change. He does it by the seasons of the year, the aging of our bodies, the alteration of our ideas, the maturing of our minds, the regeneration of our souls. The books of the Bible record one change after another—from the fertile crescent during the time of the Patriarchs to the millenial age as recorded in Revelation.

Nikos Kazantzakis, the Greek author, has written a lengthy, autobiographical account of the changes that occurred in his life—a book he entitled *Report to Greco*. It is a masterful summing-up of the events he documented to reflect the significant alterations that took place throughout his lifetime to bring him toward maturity. He was seventy-one when he began writing that book, and he died prior to its completion. The book is a rich harvest of one man's memories of a spiritual journey; a chronicle of events, carefully and sensitively recorded for himself and his readers. This quotation from chapter 17 will acquaint you with his literary style and the beauty of his writing:

> All my life one of my greatest desires has been to travel—to see and touch unknown countries, to swim in unknown seas, to circle the globe, observing new lands, seas, peoples, and ideas with insatiable appetite, to see everything for the first time and for the last time, casting a slow, prolonged glance, then to close my eyes and feel the riches deposit themselves inside me calmly or stormily according to their pleasure, until time passes them at last through its fine sieve, straining the quintessence out of all the joys and sorrows. This alchemy of the heart is, I believe, a great delight which all men deserve.[1]

As I looked at those words during my reading of *Report to Greco*, and pondered their meaning and scope, I thought a lot about that phrase, "alchemy of the heart." I looked up the word alchemy to determine its exact meaning:

> *Alchemy* n. 1. an early form of chemistry with philosophical and magical associations, studied in the Middle Ages: its chief aims were to change baser metals into gold and to discover the elixir of perpetual youth 2. a method or power of transmutation; esp., the seemingly miraculous change of a thing into something better.

As I read that definition, I realized how God had taken me through ordinary, everyday experiences and used them to teach

---

1. Nikos Kazantzakis, *Report to Greco* (New York: Bantam Books, 1971), p. 147.

me many valuable lessons about life. This journey has been, and continues to be, the alchemy of my heart. By His power and design, God has made rich deposits into my heart, calmly or stormily, according to His pleasure, allowing time to pass these deposits "through its fine sieve, straining the quintessence out of all the joys and sorrows." By means of this method He has documented His purpose for my being, thus giving my life credence and value, as well as miraculously changing "a thing into something better."

God can do this for any life. If we belong to Him, He is doing it all the time, whether we know it or not. That's His ability as the Eternal, Loving Alchemist. But it's only when we stand still, look back, and take time to reflect that we see what He has done. That's what I want to do now—stand still, look back, reflect, then record the alchemy of my heart.

Job did that in the twenty-third chapter of his book. Then he recorded this:

> But He knows the way I take;
> When He has tried me,
> I shall come forth as gold.

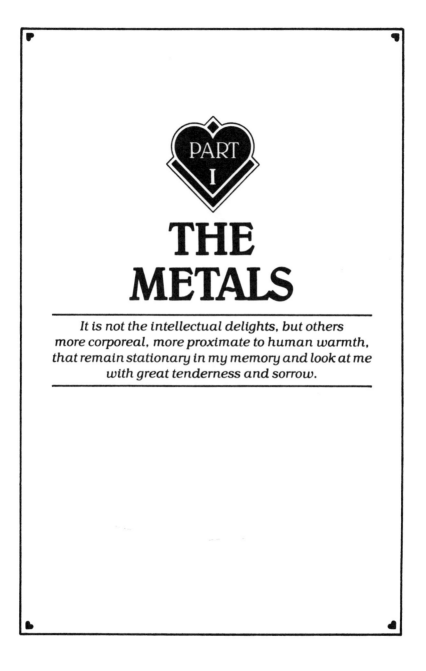

PART I

THE METALS

It is not the intellectual delights, but others more corporeal, more proximate to human warmth, that remain stationary in my memory and look at me with great tenderness and sorrow.

MY GRANDPARENTS

*Taking up my pen, I commenced to write
and to relieve myself—to give birth.*

I have a maddening habit. It is something that has bothered me since childhood, robbing me of joy and interfering with many of my best-laid plans. In fact, on occasion it is an embarrassing tendency that offends others as much as me: I cannot stay up late. All of my life I have been a "day person," functioning best upon first rising and feeling relatively secure about all decisions made in the early part of the day. As the hours move along toward noontime, afternoon, and evening, however, it is as though my metabolic rate lessens and I feel myself running down, much like a clock that has not been wound.

I hate this habit, or disposition—whichever you want to call it—because, by its very nature, it causes me to miss so much in life. When a workday is over or the chores of a Saturday are accomplished, one wants to read or visit with one's family and friends, go to a movie, a party, or perhaps watch TV . . . do any number of enjoyable things that require energy and alertness. But for me—if they are not accomplished by 9:00 P.M. I am usually "over the hill." Oh, I've tried all sorts of remedies to correct this malady but little helps. It's as though there is a tiny computer inside me, operating independently of my brain waves, which shuts off of its own accord, and to find me clear-witted and attentive at 10:00 P.M. is so unusual that my friends have been known to ask at that hour, "What are you doing up? Are you sick?"

This disappointing aspect of my temperament has reached enormously humiliating proportions, such as the time I fell asleep at a party around 9:30, long before any of the guests left—the party being given by me, at my house. Or that especially mortifying occasion when I not only dropped off into slumber on a date as my escort was driving me home, but I also began to snore. Fortunately we had become good friends by that time, as well as erstwhile sweethearts, so he was not only amused, but understanding. Nevertheless, it was embarrassing, friends . . . very embarrassing. Upon arrival in my driveway, I remember hearing his kind words, "Wake up, Luci, we're home."

The interesting thing about this "infirmity," it seems to me, is that it affects fewer people than its equally maddening counterpart, insomnia. I hear folks quite often saying, "I just couldn't sleep last night. It was awful." And I'm thinking, "Awful? Mercy! I'd love to have insomnia. Think of all I could accomplish if I could simply stay awake."

Well, about two weeks ago I was blessed with insomnia, and it was wonderful, just as I had imagined. It was a Saturday night in May, the Saturday before Mother's Day. My usual slumber hour had come and gone and—wonder of wonders—I was still awake. Wide awake. I could hardly believe it, so to celebrate this unique event I decided to enjoy a cup of hot spiced tea and listen to an opera, while I used the hours constructively to clean out an old chest of memorabilia that once belonged to my grandparents. Since I wanted music that would befit this noteworthy and unexpected occasion—the celebration of being awake while the rest of the world slept—I chose Bellini's beautiful nineteenth century opera, *La Sonnambula,* "The Sleepwalker." I thought that very appropriate as the motif for the night. So, settling down with my cup of tea in the foreground and that gorgeous music in the background, I opened the cedar chest as the clock was striking 10:30. What a memorable moment that was; I had a curious sense of victory, having won, for a change, the game of Nighttime Is for Sleeping. Little did I know then what an unforgettable night lay ahead of me.

That old chest was crammed full of things worth staying

awake to see. It was a veritable family treasure box: tattered and yellowed photographs, piles of scrapbooks, jewelry, handsewn stitchery and embroidery (everything from handkerchiefs to tablecloths), awards, letters, poetry, old Bibles, birth and death certificates, cherished books, marriage licenses, grant deeds to various pieces of property, diplomas, telegrams, greeting cards, handmade valentines and paper dolls, military documents and medals, newspaper clippings. All there. All for my eyes to behold and for my heart to render a quiet and private service of commemoration.

Piece by piece I began to take everything out, carefully unfolding visible proofs of four individuals who had, by the quality of their lives upon this earth, inexorably impacted my life. These people, my maternal and fraternal grandparents (the last of whom died twenty-three years ago), had lived, loved, hoped, lost, labored, rejoiced, yearned, struggled—felt all the same feelings I too have felt in my lifetime. The only difference was that they had experienced these feelings two generations before me.

As I summoned the past to make its presence real, I looked at old photographs of wizened faces I once touched and kissed, hands I held as a child, smiles I loved. For one dizzy, reflective moment I even thought I heard, in *La Sonnambula*, a few bars of my grandmother's pianistic interpretation of a song I used to beg her to play, called "Banjo Twang." She taught piano for over thirty years and would rip through that number with amazing dexterity as I sat in awe and wonder at her ability, only to have me excitedly say to her at the conclusion of the piece, "Do it in another key, Momo; do it in another key." And . . . she would! In my reverence for her skill I repeatedly queried, "How can you play that in so many keys?" and she would respond with a smile, "The magic of practice!"

My maternal grandmother, Jessie Lundy, or "Momo," as we affectionately called her, was truly a character. She loved to laugh and play pranks on her friends and other family members. When I was in my early teens, living in Houston, Momo would board the bus in her South Texas town and come to Houston to spend the day or the weekend with us while my grandfather was on one of his many fishing jaunts. Laughter and practical jokes would begin the moment Momo arrived, or if they didn't, something was drastically wrong. Once, and I don't recall the exact circumstances, we were taking her to the bus station on a Sunday evening for her return trip home. In a quiet moment (which was rare indeed for my family) as we were riding along in the car, Momo said, "Well, the weekend was a failure."

Somewhat shocked at this pronouncement, my father asked, "Why? I thought we had a good time."

"No," she said, "we only laughed once. That was all—what was wrong with us?" Wrong, indeed! For her, there was a value judgment regarding laughter: It was right to laugh and wrong not to. I can recall very few times when I was with her that laughter was not the most predominant sound in my ears. And when I went to bed at night, I could still hear it. That inexplicable, joyously ringing utterance crossing the sound waves of time, making one relax and think, "We're gonna make it . . . things are gonna be OK . . . we're together . . . this is fun . . . this is right!"

Coupled with her joy of living and seeing the funny side of everything—and if there wasn't one, she'd do everything in her power to create it—was a spirit filled with compassion and kindness. Catering to the underdog or the stranger, she made her house into a harbor for people, many of whom I had never seen before in my life—people who were lonely or broke or new in the community. She hated for anyone to hurt or suffer.

With her own children she felt the same. She was not the disciplinarian in the family. In fact, my mother told me once that her father, while a loving and tender man, was the only strict one of her two parents. For instance, my grandfather forbade my mother (while she was a senior in high school) to see a young man who called on her at the front door of their home one evening—an action which not only disappointed my mother but dissatisfied Momo as well. Therefore, as the young man sheepishly retreated down the front walk and my grandfather went back to his own business, Momo went out the back door, stopped the departing caller dead in his tracks, and brought him back to the house. She sneaked him in the rear entrance, where he met my mother, and the two of them had an hour's visit as my eagle-eyed grandmother kept a watchful lookout for her husband, the efficient authority of his household. (Wouldn't it be great for every teenager to have a grandmother like Momo?)

One corner of the cedar chest was covered with scrapbooks created by my grandmother's inventive and endless imagination. Pasted on every inch of every page of every book were photographs, newspaper cuttings, pressed flowers, musical programs, personal and handwritten notes, birth announcements, art work, and her own poetry. One lengthy narrative poem, entitled "The Ark," is about a closet in her home, chockfull of all the paraphernalia she kept on hand "just in case" she wanted to throw one of her famous parties. Among other things, the poem mentions tents, army cots, stools, hats, socks, halltrees, umbrellas, fans, puttees, spats, bunting, croquet balls and mallets, rugs, stoves, ties, paper flowers, curtains, lace, shotguns, violins, chimes, bugles, jazz bows, graduation hats, jack-o'-lanterns, and toys.

I am absolutely certain that within a three or four hour period my dear old grandmother could have arranged a masquerade party or a fancy wedding (and sometimes there is little difference between the two) with a fully decorated house and one hundred guests. She was truly the best of the big-time party givers. Being in her company and watching her operate in all realms of outreach was my first conscious exposure to a preschool education. Her unintentional teaching was, I believe, God's initial tilling of the soil of my fertile, childish heart for future cultivation. She was my role model and heroine.

I loved her deeply until the day she died in January, 1953, and I'll never forget the moment I heard she had passed away. It was about five o'clock in the evening. I was in the music building of the college I was attending at the time, practicing for a vocal concert with the glee club. We were rehearsing a marvelous piece from Mozart's *Requiem Mass*, the "Lacrimosa," meaning "Tears," which was, incidentally, the last piece of music Mozart wrote. The messenger (a girl who informed me that my father was on the phone in my dorm with a death message regarding my grandmother) said, "He's waiting for you to come to the phone; he wants to talk to you."

As I left the building, hardly able to comprehend what she had said, "something about death . . . and my grandmother . . ." long evening shadows were falling across the campus and I was running toward the telephone with the music of Mozart fading behind me in the distance:

> Ah! That day of tears and mourning!
> From the dust of earth returning,
> Man for judgment must prepare him.
> Spare, O God, in mercy spare him!
> Lord, all pitying, Jesu blest,
> Grant them Thine eternal rest. Amen.

How true! The choir was vocalizing Momo's entrance into God's eternal rest. I held one of her scrapbooks in my hands thirty years later, while the memory and joy of her presence flooded over me again, as though she were right there sitting beside me.

With the same conviction that I would label my grandmother a character, I must call her husband, my grandfather, a saint. He epitomized this quotation:

> Why were the saints, saints? Because they were cheerful when it was difficult to be cheerful, patient when it was difficult to be patient; and because they pushed on when they wanted to stand still, and kept silent when they wanted to talk, and were agreeable when they wanted to be disagreeable. That was all. It was quite simple and it always will be.

Granddaddy was a simple man—simple in dress and manner, simple in habits and practices, and simple in his style of living. Actually it was his wife who brought the verve and imagination to his life. But don't think for a moment that he was dull. He wasn't. He was busy and preoccupied with his duties, which seemed to be legion. This man, Orville Lundy, was not only a husband and father of four children, but he owned the largest insurance agency in the Texas town in which his family lived, and he was justice of the peace and legal magistrate in the county, with the authority to decide minor court cases, commit persons to trial in a higher court, and perform marriages. Granddaddy taught the men's Bible class in his church for forty years and was infinitely well respected among his peers and friends.

And . . . he was a crackerjack fisherman. I have known him on many occasions to call or write my father to meet him at the bay for a day or weekend of fishing, or . . . to fish alone for hours in an effort to work through a problem or find solace at a time when he was disquieted in his soul. While mulling over an issue, making an important decision, or mentally writing his Bible lesson, he would at the same time catch a "mess of fish." He had a sixth sense about where to drop anchor. And fishing, to him, was not only a pastime, it was a skill to be mastered and utilized for all of life. Where my grandmother needed people to work through her problems, Granddaddy required solitude. However, the time both of them spent in their respective realms of preference brought the same result: contentment.

Of the generation of ancestors whom I personally knew, Granddaddy was the last to die. As I sat there in the stillness of that memorial tribute to my grandparents, I recalled an event which took place between him and me about five years before his death. I had graduated from college and gotten my first job. I had acquired a position as an art teacher at an orphanage in Texas. I was thrilled with the chance to "make my mark" in life, but I was also very green when it came to experience and taking responsibility for my own actions. Granddaddy, the wise and generous person that he was, decided to help me get started with things by floating me a reasonable loan to buy my first car. It was about $700, if I recall correctly, so he and I looked around until I found just what I wanted—a "darling" 1952 Chevy, green and spiffy. Both of us were pleased with the purchase, and in Granddaddy's characteristic eagerness for me to learn a sense of responsibility, he charged me $25 per month plus a small interest. Nothing exorbitant and well within the bounds of a sound budget—had I had the good sense to live on a budget. But I didn't, of course. Here I was, a wealthy woman of twenty-three, a college graduate with my first job and my own car, spending money right and left. When one gets out of college where one has lived four years on an allowance of $20 a month, an orphanage teacher's salary looks something like the annual earnings of one of the Rockefellers. Gigantic!

Before too many months, my style of spending not only depleted my monthly earnings but payday became "exchange day." I was head over heels in debt. Fortunately, I had begun regularly and consistently to reimburse Granddaddy for his generous loan, but I still owed him $500 when I began to realize there was no way I could continue that payment to him of $25 plus interest a month. So . . . you guessed it—the payments stopped. Here was my immature and presumptuous rationale: "He's my grandfather; he'll understand. He probably doesn't expect it anyway because he's old, and old people always have money stashed away in the mattress or someplace. When I get out of debt I'll send him the rest, but right now I need it a lot more than he does. I'll just explain it to him and he'll say, 'Forget it, honey, I don't need it anyway. Let's make the last $500 a gift.' This $25 a month probably goes unnoticed by Granddaddy."

With that thought in mind, I stopped the payments. But ironically enough, my debts got worse instead of better. Every month it was something new to handle financially. Weeks passed and I didn't write Granddaddy to explain the situation. Then months passed with no word from him. After a while I thought, "Well, gosh! How can I tell him now? I already owe him for so many back payments that it's too embarrassing to write. I'll just let it go." But . . . the Spirit of God in my heart wouldn't let it go. That $25 a month plagued my steps for weeks and months and finally for years. All the while my grandfather *never* mentioned it to me, nor to my parents, I assume. Little did he know, however, that I was never without the worm of guilt boring its way into the core of my very active conscience.

During this time, my minister spoke one Sunday from Romans 13 on responsibility's being a part of maturity. The explanation of practically every verse convicted my grieving spirit. Words like: "Render to all what is due them . . . owe nothing to anyone . . . and this do, knowing the time, that it is already the hour for you to awaken from sleep . . . let us behave properly . . ." Every word leaped from the page and grabbed me by the throat. (Nobody can tell me that the Holy Spirit doesn't convict of wrong-doing!) Finally I had had enough of myself and my laxity regarding this financial responsibility.

The very next day, early Monday morning, I went to the credit union of the company where I worked and took out a loan for $500. With the check in my hand, I went immediately to the bank, deposited it, and wrote a personal check to my grandfather with a long overdue, sincere note of regret for my actions and a request for his forgiveness. That was the last time I ever borrowed money (large or small) from a family member or anyone else. From then on, all of my loans were handled through a lending institution. I had at least learned that one lesson, if nothing else. But God wasn't quite through with the larger scope of what He wanted to teach me.

About a week later I received a note from my grandfather in somewhat scribbled handwriting. He thanked me for the money without one word of chiding, and reported that he had not been feeling very good and was grateful to have the extra funds in order to handle some escalating medical expenses. Then he closed with his love and his best regards for my health and my future. The note was concise, but very sweet. Matter of fact but understanding—just like Granddaddy did things.

Two weeks later he was dead.

I suffered enormously in my soul. A dichotomous battle raged inside me for months; in some ways I rejoiced that I had gotten my debt paid off before he died, but in other ways I agonized over my own inexcusable tardiness in waiting so long. I'm not inexperienced enough to believe that receiving that $500 earlier could have saved his life, but I do know that my years of carrying around such a grievous fault could have been shortened and eliminated had I just taken hold of the obligation that was mine. In my mind, his sainthood increased in brilliance a hundredfold, especially as it was reflected off my own darkened heart which had been consciously living in disobedience for so long a time. On the last page of that scrapbook there was a snapshot of Granddaddy and me standing in front of my old '52 Chevy. The picture had been taken shortly after I had bought the car. I looked at it carefully, thinking, "Strange . . . there we are, the two of us, standing in front of the very vehicle that God used to get my attention, to force me to start being responsible for my own life."

When I closed the book, everything seemed deathly still and quiet. The music had stopped. My teacup was empty. I looked at my watch and it was 2:20 A.M. What a night for insomnia. I was loving it but I could feel my body beginning to get tired for the first time. It was Sunday morning by now and I knew I needed sleep, so I picked up a small Bible that had belonged to my father's mother, Lillian Swindoll, and a yellowed letter dated May 5, 1927 and took them to bed with me to read before finally turning off my light.

I opened the Bible to the first page, where my father had written these words:

> This Bible was given to my mother (whose maiden name was Lillie Beatrice Leigh) on December 25, 1883.

It was signed in my father's beautiful, expressive handwriting, "Earl L. Swindoll."

Under that was printed:

> Given to Lucille Swindoll by her mother and father, November 25, 1969 (Dallas, Texas).

I held the Bible for a while, flipping through its pages, wishing I had known my father's parents. My grandfather, Charles Swindoll, died before I was born, and my grandmother died when I was a small girl of eight or nine, so I never had the privilege of knowing either of them. As I turned pages, I looked for markings or underlinings that would tell me something about my grandmother, but I found only one verse that had been marked. There was a penciled arrow pointing to Isaiah 25:8:

He will swallow up death in victory; and the Lord God will wipe away tears from off all faces; and the rebuke of his people shall he take away from off all the earth: for the Lord hath spoken it.

Then I thought, "That's right. I may not know them now, but I will someday." I set the old Bible on my night table and opened the letter. It had been written by my dad to his mother when he was thirty-four.

Raton, New Mexico
May 5, 1927

My dear Mother,

I just wanted to write you a few lines and let you know that you should receive on "Mother's Day" a hanging basket as a remembrance.

As I grow older each year, I can appreciate all the more what a wonderful mother you have been and my love for you grows dearer and sweeter each day. As I glance back over only a few years I can see the many deeds of lovingkindness that I have received from you and can feel that keenness of a mother's love for her boy.

Am enclosing a clipping from the Santa Fe Magazine which I think is just fine and I knew you would love to read it—how true every word! And if every boy could only know that his mother is just that much interested in him, I am quite sure there would be lots better men in the world today. So many men no doubt are so busy in life that they forget that all they have and are comes from a mother's love—but I shall never get so busy that I will forget for one moment that I have a mother who has been everything to me.

I realize there are times when mothers think their sons have forgotten but I know that deep down in every boy's heart is a "big" warm spot that never ceases to remember the love for his mother.

I only trust that someday I can prove to you that I am everything that you had hoped I would be when I grew up to be a man.

Did you get the three spools of thread? Don't send any money for it as I still owe you some from the last time I sent you thread.

Well, I must say goodbye again now. Write me when you feel like it and tell me about your hanging basket.

Lots of love and kisses for "mother's day."

> Lovingly,
> Your son, Earl

When I turned off the light, I realized it *was* Mother's Day—fifty-six years later.

MY FATHER

*I never forgot that moment. I believe that it served
as a great lesson in the crises of my life.
I always remembered my father standing calmly,
motionlessly on the threshold . . . motionless
he stood watching. . . .*

J ust as my grandmother became my heroine because of
all she got out of living, my father became my hero because of all he put into it. For eighty-seven years he
gave life his best shot! My dad, Earl L. Swindoll, was a
man of many strengths and few weaknesses. He was a devoted
and faithful husband to my mother for forty years and a loving
father to my two brothers and me until he died. Because of his
natural ability to lead, coupled with a quiet, patient demeanor,
one felt secure in his presence, whether that was within his family circle, on the job, or among his friends. His behavior always
spoke of a man who was a person of character, a defender of justice, a tower of strength, a respecter of authority, a protector of
principles, and a sensitive gentleman. Could one look for any
better qualities in a hero?

What makes a person like this? If there were some magic
formula that could be patented and sold, I am certain every
father in the world who had any fears about being a competent
leader or a considerate man of honor would buy the product and
apply it daily. Unfortunately, life's best attributes do not come
that way. They are drawn out of the raw material of suffering,
loss, distress, and hurt, and then woven together with the joys
and blessings of life into a tapestry of highly esteemed character
traits. At least this was the case with my dad.

Daddy was born September 3, 1892, the first child of very loving but strict parents. His younger brother, Charles, the only other child in the family, was born four years later, but died in his early twenties in a car accident four months after returning home from active military duty in France during World War I. Due to his father's illness which lasted almost a dozen years until his death, Daddy quit high school after finishing the eleventh grade to go to a business college in order to learn a trade and help support the family. He spent one year studying bookkeeping and typing and four years becoming a journeyman machinist. During this time he began working for the Atchison, Topeka and Santa Fe Railway Company, advancing annually over the next fifteen years to more and more responsible positions. He also married and had his first child, a son. This marriage ended in divorce, with his wife being awarded custody of the son, whom he loved dearly.

Upon resignation from the railway company, my father began a new career in the insurance profession, for which he received training through correspondence courses. He actively and wholeheartedly pursued this career for the following fifteen years. He was recognized as the most outstanding salesman in the company for nine of those years. During this period he and my mother met and married. She was twenty-three. He was thirty-eight. Three children were born of that union—my older brother, Orville, my younger brother, Charles, and myself. Daddy was forty years old in September of 1932 when I was born that same month.

In 1942 my dad, at the age of fifty, became an inspector with the United States Army Air Force. His annual salary at that age was exactly twelve times less than mine is today, at the same age. He worked long and hard hours, overtime, and night shifts, and he received excellent efficiency ratings and appraisals, all of which I have kept and treasure. After sixteen continuously active months in this capacity, Daddy had a severe breakdown in his health which resulted in his need for much rest. I don't remember his reporting to work for almost two years, a very long time for a man with such a strong work ethic.

In June, 1947, Daddy began working for the "Cleco" division of Reed Roller Bit Company in Houston and remained with them until his retirement in 1957, at the age of sixty-five. He never officially stopped working, however, until much later. When he was seventy-two, he and mother sold their home in Houston and moved to Dallas, where they managed apartments for the next four years. In my file drawer labeled "Important Papers," I have a copy of his last employment application which he filled out in 1973, in his strong and inimitable handwriting, but later wrote on the front, "never used." He was eighty-one.

That same year he took his first plane flight—to another country to visit his older son Orville and his family—and the following year he moved to another state to live with Charles, his younger son.

In 1920, my father became a Freemason. He was active in this endeavor for thirty-seven years. In 1953 he became an interested student of the Bible and read it daily until a year before his death, when he could no longer hold it in his hands. He was a conservative from the day he was able to vote, and an extremely patriotic American all his life.

Now, you ask, why is this detail so important? Because . . . woven throughout Daddy's life is the continual thread of a personal pursuit toward excellence. I have attempted to show in this chronology his ever-constant desire to meet the challenge, to be the very best he could be, striving always to better himself, never allowing difficulties, heartaches, or personal disappointments to hold him back. As I said in the opening paragraph of this chapter, he gave life his best shot—always.

If a person is like this within himself, if his desire is to be the best he can be, he not only sees the immediate problems and seeks to correct them, but he reaches beyond those to an even higher calling. And . . . he is inclined to encourage those about him to reach for something higher as well. Truthfully, I cannot remember a time I went to my father with a problem related to discouragement that he not only helped me with it but offered me sound advice in greater matters, too. And he always did it in such a supportive, affirming way. For example, I remember having terrible problems in math (the bane of my existence) and talking to my dad about this. I told him I was no good with figures, that I didn't like math, that I was a failure, etc. He listened quietly, looking at me, appraising my face and trying to ascertain the depth of my insecurity. Then he said:

> Honey, first of all, you are NOT a failure. Even if you tried, you could never be a failure because you're a Swindoll. Being a Swindoll means you're a winner. You have a good mind and you have a good memory. Maybe you're just a little lazy or you're not concentrating—but you can lick this problem. You've got to apply yourself. I'll work with you and we'll lick it together. OK? And most important of all, you have the Lord. With the Lord, it's impossible for you to fail. Don't ever forget it. Now, what's the math problem? . . .

Then we'd work on it together. I learned the entire set of multiplication tables in the evenings as I washed the dinner dishes and Daddy dried them. And you know what? It was fun. One of the most fun activities my dad and I ever "licked" together.

Or there was the occasion I was afraid to speak before an audience or sing a solo for the first time. He'd say, "You can do it, honey. I know you can! Just go out there and be natural—be yourself. If anybody else can do it, you can do it, too . . . maybe even better." Oh, the times I've heard that from him. Even now, so many decades later, when I get ready to tackle a new problem I hear his loving voice saying, "If anybody else can do it, you can do it too . . . maybe even better."

Those kinds of encouraging remarks build confidence in a child. And I will venture to say that numerous battles my brothers and I fight and win through the years begin with hearing those words in our heads from Daddy. We simply start out by thinking if anybody else can do it, we can too, and before we get into the deep water of uncertainties and fears, faith enters the picture, God charts the course, and it is humanly too embarrassing to turn back. That seems to be the way some of the biggest projects work out for me. I start with those four little words: YOU CAN DO IT, and before long, it gets done. Who can explain it? As a dear friend of mine said to me once, "Luci, the reason you get involved in so many things is because your father never told you you couldn't," and I suppose that's true.

Humanly speaking, of course, there are countless limitations, but the principle of one's pursuit toward excellence has no boundaries. Our outreach and accomplishments are as narrow as we think they will be. And, generally, when they are broad they are much broader than we ever dream, because once our faith is activated, God honors it and takes over. Then . . . the sky's the limit. I learned that from my father. He was committed, I believe, to teaching everybody he met that truth—that concept—and he was intentional about that commitment. On "Career Day," April 14, 1955, my dad was asked to give a speech at the high school I had attended and from which I had graduated five years before. His particular area of expertise being machine shop, it was to those students he delivered his address. It was full of challenges, enthusiasm, and encouragement, and no less than five times in that speech Daddy used the phrase, "If you want to enough." He talked about the importance of learning, applying knowledge to experience, not being satisfied with a sloppy job, being loyal to a task and a company, and always growing in every field of endeavor. In short, he left his audience with the thought that excellence does not fall into one's lap. It must be sought after and earned.

But learning to pursue excellence was certainly not the only thing my dad taught me, and perhaps not even the best thing out of his many important principles for living. While I received the former rules of conduct from Daddy's attentive performance to his fatherly duties—or his "commission," so to speak—I learned a greater foundational principle from his "omission" of duties.

It all ties into an incident which occurred when I was twelve. We were living in Houston at the time and I was in junior high school. At this point in my life I had just enough knowledge of living to realize that experience was only beginning for me and just enough knowledge of scripture to be dangerous. In other words, I was the epitome of a legalistic kid. I had begun to memorize verses, witness to my friends, fervently proclaim the Lord's return with every passing day, and generally believe that all things regarding life were absolutely black or absolutely white. No middle ground. No gray areas. None. Ever been around people like that? They're awful . . . and I was worse because of this aforementioned assertiveness training of which I spoke. I'm sure I was an unadulterated pain in the patootie!

Well, one evening my mother and dad had gone out to dinner with friends, a couple who lived nearby and who occasionally joined my parents for Mexican food at their favorite restaurant when we kids were involved in our own evening's activities. Such was the case that night. While they were gone, I was cleaning my bedroom, putting away some things that were out of place, and in the course of this activity I found I needed to return a book on salesmanship to a file drawer of my father's. Since I knew where it belonged, I opened the drawer and removed what was on top so I could put the book away properly (ever "Miss Prim"). After placing the book where it belonged, I lifted the other items to return them to the drawer and a piece of paper fell from the stack. It looked like some kind of contract and had the word "divorce" printed on it. I looked at it quizzically for a moment; then my curiosity got the better of me, so I set the stack of things down and unfolded the document. I could hardly believe my eyes . . . my father, divorced? Impossible. Christians don't divorce! How could this be? There must be some mistake. But there was his name in bold letters, as well as the name of some woman I had never heard of before in my life. I felt awful. My stomach turned and I felt cheated somehow. The perfect, flawless, omniscient father that I adored and revered was divorced. I put the paper away, stacked the other items on top of it, and shut the drawer. Tears started streaming down my face and I went to my room and cried. My heart felt broken. I was furious with Daddy as I kept seeing the words of that legal document of divorce flash onto my mind's eye.

Mother and Daddy came home and, as was their custom, greeted us warmly. I didn't look up. I sat there at my bedroom desk with my back to the door, as though I were reading and doing my homework. They didn't linger, but went on about their evening's business. Later I got ready for bed, carrying around a rock in my stomach and the world's heaviest heart. My dad came to my room and asked me if I was all right.

"Yeah, fine," I said.

He stood at the threshold of the doorway, very still, calmly looking at me, waiting for me to look him in the eyes. "Honey," he said, "what's wrong? Are you OK?" I didn't say anything. I'm sure he wanted to force me to talk, but that wasn't his way. He waited and watched me but did not insist that I say anything.

After a minute or two he came into the room and sat down on my bed. When he opened his mouth to speak, I blurted out, "Daddy, have you been drinking beer? Do I smell beer on your breath?"

He looked at me and very calmly answered, "Yes, honey, I had a beer with dinner tonight . . . why?"

That did it! I burst into tears, told him about finding the paper of divorcement, how I hated him for not telling me he had been married before, and now to find out he actually drank beer. In all my childish seriousness I announced that I was certain he was going straight to hell and that until that moment I had always thought he was the most wonderful man who ever lived, but from then on I *never* wanted to speak to him again.

He didn't say anything, but I could see his eyes getting watery. He tried to reach out and embrace me, but I wouldn't have it. I said, "Don't touch me, Daddy. Leave me alone—just leave me alone."

Finally he stood up, walked to the door, stood there looking so sweetly and softly at me. Then very quietly he said, "I love you . . ." and turned, walked out, and went to bed.

For three days I did not utter a word to my father. I had privately declared a moratorium on communication and affection . . . and he never once made me speak or chided me for my silent and resentful behavior. He just looked at me with love and regret that he seemed to have no ability to change the circumstances. He actually let me pout, and waited for time to heal the breach between us.

Eventually my feelings came back into realistic perspective and my heart mellowed, but for many months I carried that occurrence in my active thoughts, even after Daddy explained the circumstances surrounding his first marriage and subsequent divorce as well as informing me that he had had a son in that marriage. He stated his reasons for not giving me this information earlier and he sought to clarify the confusion that my legalistic viewpoint produced. He encouraged me to try not to "spiritualize" everything that happens in life; that there are many issues that will never be totally black or white, but are dependent upon numerous other factors I was too young to understand at the time. And as he was conveying this information to me, he let me ask any question I wanted, expose any uncertainty I had, blow off any steam that had accumulated. Throughout the entire conversation I felt his warmth, tolerance, sincerity, affection, patience, and even his touch of humor. That may not be the way you would handle that problem and perhaps not even the best way. But who's to say what's always "best" in relationship misunderstandings? That was Daddy's way and his tolerance affected me for life.

I am certain that the idealistic demands I placed upon my dad to perform in a prescribed way during those days brought him a great deal of personal pain and heartache. I wanted him to be without flaws. I wanted the epitome of perfection. Oh, how stupid I was—and it cost me three precious days of close fellowship that I'd give anything to have now. But of course it's too late.

On February 15, 1976, my dad suffered a stroke in church. I was sitting next to him while his son Charles was preaching. From that moment on, his life was never the same again. I did everything I could to relieve his problems with pain or heartache or loneliness, but the majority of my time was spent in handling his bodily needs rather than in the father-daughter communication and fellowship we had known and loved for the previous forty-four years. I had been with him in his hospital room only a few hours before he died, a frail, quiet man of eighty-seven, and his final words to me were "I love you"—just like that night, thirty-six years before, when he spoke those words and then turned from my bedroom door.

My brothers loved Daddy as much as I. Upon the occasion of his death, we each wrote a tribute to him in our own way. Chuck's has been published in a book he has written, *Make Up Your Mind . . . About the Issues of Life.* Orville's tribute was in a letter to me, and mine was a note to Daddy, written a few days after his burial. I quote each one here as a final, collected acknowledgment of thanksgiving to our father—a man whose enormous contribution to our lives far surpasses any of these words.

From Chuck:

My dad died last night.

He left like he had lived. Quietly. Graciously. With dignity. Without demands or harsh words or even a frown, he surrendered himself—a tired, frail, humble gentleman—into the waiting arms of his Savior. Death, selfish and cursed enemy of man, won another battle.

As I stroked the hair from his forehead and kissed him goodbye, a hundred boyhood memories played around in my head.

When I learned to ride a bike, he was there.

When I wrestled with the multiplication table, his quick wit erased the hassle.

When I discovered the adventure of driving a car, he was near, encouraging me.

When I got my first job (delivering newspapers), he informed me how to increase my subscriptions and win the prize. It worked!

When I mentioned a young woman I had fallen in love with, he pulled me aside and talked straight about being responsible for her welfare and happiness.

When I did a hitch in the Marine Corps, the discipline I had learned from him made the transition easier.

From him I learned to seine for shrimp. How to catch flounder and trout and red fish. How to open oyster shells and fix crab gumbo . . . and chili . . . and popcorn . . . and make rafts out of old inner tubes and gunny sacks. I was continually amazed at his ability to do things like tie fragile mantles on the old Coleman lantern, keep a fire going in the rain, play the harmonica with his hands behind his back, and keep three strong-willed kids from tearing the house down.

Last night I realized I had him to thank for my deep love for America. And for knowing how to tenderly care for my wife. And for laughing at impossibilities. And for some of the habits I have picked up, like approaching people with a positive spirit rather than a negative one, staying with a task until it is finished, taking good care of my personal belongings, keeping my shoes shined, speaking up rather than mumbling, respecting authority, and standing alone (if necessary) in support of my personal convictions rather than giving in to more popular opinions. For these things I am deeply indebted to the man who raised me.

Certain smells and sounds now instantly remind me of my dad. Oyster stew. The ocean breeze. Smoke from an expensive cigar. The nostalgic whine of a harmonica. A camping lantern and white gas. Car polish. Fun songs from the 30s and 40s. Freshly mowed grass. A shrill whistle from a father to his kids around supper time. And Old Spice aftershave.

Because a father impacts his family so permanently, I think I understand better than ever what the Scripture means when Paul wrote:

> Having thus a fond affection for you, we were well-pleased to impart to you not only the gospel of God but also our own lives, because you had become very dear to us. . . . just as you know how we were exhorting and encouraging and imploring each one of you as a father would his own children, so that you may walk in a manner worthy of the God who calls you into His own kingdom and glory (1 Thessalonians 2:8, 11-12).

Admittedly, much of my dad's instruction was indirect—by model rather than by explicit statement. I do not recall his overt declarations of love as clearly as I do his demonstrations of it. His life revolved around my mother, the darling and delight of his life. Of that I am sure. When she left over nine years ago, something of him died as well. And so—to her he has been joined and they are, together, with our Lord. In the closest possible companionship one can imagine.

In this my sister, my brother, and I find our greatest comfort—they are now forever with the Lord—eternally freed from pain and aging and death. Secure in Jesus Christ our Lord. Absent from the body and at home with Him. And with each other.

Last night I said goodbye. I'm still trying to believe it. You'd think it would be easy since his illness had persisted for more than three years. How well I remember the Sunday he suffered that first in a series of strokes as I was preaching. God granted him several more years to teach many of us to appreciate the things we tend to take for granted.

He leaves in his legacy a well-marked Bible I treasure, a series of feelings that I need to deepen my roots, and a thousand memories that comfort me as I replace denial with acceptance and praise.

I await heaven's gate opening in the not-too-distant future. So do other Christians, who anxiously await Christ's return. Most of them anticipate hearing the soft strum of a harp or the sharp, staccato blast of a trumpet.

Not me. I will hear the nostalgic whine of a harmonica . . . held in the hands of the man who died last night . . . or did he? The memories are as fresh as this morning's sunrise.[1]

From Orville:

> Buenos Aires, Argentina
> March 28, 1980

Dearest Sis,

According to my calculations (5 P.M. Dallas time, 8 P.M. here), I suppose Dad's funeral is now almost over and a chapter

---

1. Charles R. Swindoll, *Make Up Your Mind . . . About the Issues of Life* (Portland, Oreg.: Multnomah Press, 1981), pp. 90-91.

has closed on our lives. My thoughts, since you called yesterday, have often turned to so many fond memories of Dad's calm composure, clear authority and strong sense of fatherhood which he so effectively communicated to us. I think of how foolishly I sometimes chafed under his stern sense of justice and his determination that we be raised to glorify God and bring honor to the Swindoll name. At this juncture in my life all those values seem so very important that my heart can only find gratitude and honor for his excellent leadership and for the strong sense of spiritual, human and moral values he instilled in us.

While I feel there was no great and overriding reason that I should have made the long trip in order to be present at his interment, I sense a bit of remorse for not having been there, if only to honor him in his death and exalt his memory for those values which are so frequently ill-esteemed or even mocked in so much of today's society. In the memory of my mind, Dad will always be to me a bulwark of strength, a fortress of moral fiber in a wasteland of humanistic relativism. His logical arguments, his strong sense of right and justice were so balanced with a respect for human dignity and a love for life in general, that he indelibly and inexorably impressed upon the character of all his children the same basic value judgments. All of these strong characteristics so heavily outweighed his minor negative traits, that I have real difficulty even remembering things about him which I would classify as faults.

I rejoice over the assurance that he has now gone to his eternal reward, and will suffer no more. The Lord gave him a good, long and fruitful life and a very enjoyable one. We had our dad around a lot longer than many have.

> Gratefully yours,
> Orville and family

My Father

From me:

April 1, 1980

My Dearest Daddy,

Four days ago we took your "earthly remains" to Dallas for burial, and now, while your soul and spirit are enjoying eternal happiness with our Lord and with Mother (who was the true love of your life), your bones lie in that little burial plot awaiting the day of resurrection when those graves are going to open up. Who knows, maybe my bones will be there too, since that third spot is designated for my "remains."

Remember how you and I used to talk about 1 Corinthians 2:9? You always loved that verse and had it well marked in your Bible:

> But it is written, eye hath not seen, nor ear heard, neither have entered into the heart of man, the things which God hath prepared for them that love him.

And to think—now you know all those things from experience because you're there with your Savior.

I will miss you, Daddy. So much! I have loved you deeply all my life, and you have been the finest example of a father any human being could want. Didn't we have great times, though? Remember that evening (about nine years ago) when we started out for a wedding, and because we were early, we stopped in a coffee shop for a quick cup of coffee (dressed to the teeth, of course, because we were supposed to be going to a wedding)? After we got seated it began to rain. It poured cats and dogs for an hour, and we finally decided we'd skip the wedding and stay at the coffee shop all evening. So we ordered bacon and eggs (to go with the coffee)—sat there all dressed up, laughed, re-lived old times and had a great evening. Remember, you said, "I wonder if these waitresses think we always dress like this when we go out for coffee?" After about three hours, when the rain subsided, we drove home, wedding gift still in the car.

And that was only one of hundreds of laugh-filled times that have been ours. You were truly a funny man, Daddy, and oh! so much more: loving, sweet, generous, gracious, witty, charming, etc., etc. The list goes on. You were, in my opinion, a great father in every sense of the word, and you certainly knew how to handle me and my problems. How did you always know? It seems your vast experience, together with your knowledge of scripture, made you able to handle anything.

Thank you, Daddy, for the gift of loving affection these past forty-seven years and for your unceasing devotion to such high moral standards. I know there are going to be times I will want to talk with you or seek your counsel . . . but I'll have to rely on what you've taught me all these years. I won't forget what's important . . . I promise.

You're better off now, anyway, Dad. I wouldn't have you back even if I could—but for one exception. Do you recall when I was a twelve-year-old, narrow-minded brat? And I wouldn't speak to you for three days because I found out you were divorced *and* that you drank beer? Horror of horrors! Oh, Daddy, I would do those days differently in a minute if given the chance. I am still deeply sorry for my immature, intolerant actions. And you were so patient and kind—just like always.

Yes. I'd have those days back. I would apologize over and over and we'd go to your favorite Mexican restaurant to celebrate our reunion. And . . . you know what, Daddy? I'd even have a beer with you.

> I love you,
> Luci

MY MOTHER

As in love, so in hospitality, surely
he who gives is happier than he who receives.

"**W**ell, today I finished memorizing the book of 1 Peter," she said to me that night at dinner.

"You did what?"

"I finished memorizing 1 Peter," Mother repeated. "For the past few weeks in church, Charles has been encouraging all the members to get busy and memorize scripture, so I figured he probably meant me, too, even though I am his mother. Today I finished learning the last seven verses. Want me to quote them for you?"

I said, "Wait a minute, Mother. You couldn't mean you memorized that entire book. Why, there are a jillion verses in the book of 1 Peter."

"One hundred and five," she said, smiling. "I can do the after dinner floor show tonight by quoting the book of 1 Peter. I need the practice."

"Oh, Mother, that's *great.* I can hardly believe it. I may know four or five verses from that book, and here you are, a sixty-year-old woman, memorizing the whole thing."

"Sixty-one."

I laughed. "Whatever. You know how I am with figures. Why didn't you pick a book with fewer verses, like 3 John or Jude? That's more my speed."

"I don't know. It's just that 1 Peter has so much good teaching that will help us today. Things like God's grace—His graciousness and care toward us. The value of humility, the promise that God will bless us when we are patient during suffering, how the gospel endures forever. All those good things. Besides, Charles told me he had memorized 1 Peter, so I thought if he could do it, I could too."

After dinner that evening my father and I sat in the living room, transfixed, as my sixty-one-year-old, gray-haired mother, Lovell Swindoll, let those great verses roll off her tongue, one after another, all 105 of them. Not only were they correct and in proper order (I was holding her Bible, "checking her out," as she requested), but they were expressed with such conviction and belief—full of meaning.

Now, it is doubtful, upon hearing the above account, that in the mind of my average reader there could be any thought other than, "Luci's mother must have been an extremely mature Christian, memorizing books of the Bible and all . . ." That is true. She was a mature Christian, but you must remember that I was referring to Mother at the age of sixty-one, near the end of her life (she died at sixty-three), after God had taken her through numerous stages of development, seasoning her and refining her disposition and attitudes. Through the years He simplified her expectations. He turned the bitter to sweet, the disappointments to joys, and the disapprovals to acceptance. So before we discuss her maturity, let's take a quantum leap backward and examine a few of the factors that contributed to this development.

In my recollection and mental analysis of Mother's life, there were three obvious strikes against her from the beginning. First of all, not only did she emerge from a shielded Christian environment, but she lived her adult life in one as well. Having been reared in an economically comfortable home, she enjoyed the benefits of high breeding, and few, if any, needs went unattended. Her parents, whom we met in chapter 1, loved her, wanted her, and provided amply for all of her physical, material, and spiritual requirements. She lived with them until she went away to a Christian college. When she married my father, who adored her, she never once worked outside the home, was never gainfully employed. During the forty years they were married, the battles and struggles of her heart were the result of her own private, personal contradictions or family squabbles, with each conflict being waged in the arena of home life only. In that sense, it was as though Mother lived in a sterile cocoon, never experiencing the larger confrontations of life which result from exposure to the "slings and arrows" exhibited in the workaday world. While this is not calamitous, of course, it does tend to foster a very narrow point of view as well as somewhat inflexible horizons.

Second, the antithesis of Mother's creative and imaginative temperament was her tremendous moodiness. It was as though the gift of creativity and artistic sensibilities could not be had for nothing—they cost a great deal; they demanded sacrifices. Her sacrifice often came in the loss of congeniality. She gave up one for the other. I have seen her on more than one occasion go down the hall, walk into her bedroom, slam the door behind her, and stay there for hours, pouting over something one of us had said or left unsaid, had done or left undone. In retrospect, I'm sure that within Mother's psyche she did this because she simply did not know what else to do. It didn't solve anything, of course, but it did enable her brittle temperament to get out of the fray, which provided her the space she needed to cope. She meant no harm, I'm sure, and no punishment upon those of us left standing there, victims of her sullenness, feeling guilty for a crime we had not committed. (Perhaps you know the feeling!) Notwithstanding this fact, the mental picture of Mother closing that door is etched in my mind forever.

The third distinctive is one that largely affected only me, since I was the other female in our nucleus family. But it had great bearing upon how I was reared and understood. Mother was excessively domestic; therefore her goals for her daughter were the same. She was a marvelous cook and her pièce de résistance usually found its source in the kitchen. In this sphere of operation she enjoyed her greatest significance. Each summer she canned peaches, figs, strawberries, blackberries, and all winter our dinner table was laden with the fruit of her labor—literally. She was an excellent seamstress and a speed demon when it came to knitting or crocheting. Her needlepoint was flawless. She hand painted china as fast as she bought the blank pieces. In short, her endless domestic skills were highly developed and enjoyed by all the family. The only thing that was not enjoyed was the insistence that I be domestic, too.

I don't know what it was about me exactly, but I found so much of that scene boring, especially when I was a teenager or early college age. Maybe I viewed it as appallingly pedestrian for one who entertained the dreams and visions that I had: going to college, pursuing a career, singing professionally, traveling. In truth, I don't think it was the domesticity that I found unimaginative; rather, it was the fact that I felt I had to conform to that "calling" and reform my own high-flown ambitions. In any event, Mother's attention to household affairs seemed to negate or at least subordinate all other activities. Consequently, when I voiced my desires for future development to her, if they deviated from home, hearth, or family, she often misunderstood them or gave them insufficient credence. Alas! In this context, I was unconsciously fighting for my own autonomy; a condition, it seemed to me, that the males of the family already possessed simply by virtue of the fact they were male. I think it is safe to say that the frequent major disagreements Mother and I experienced sprung by and large from this basic difference in our goals.

Let me hasten to add here that the other side of Mother's personality makeup was a shining contrast. In these areas I was her greatest cheerleader! No one could have been more fond of entertaining nor have more genuinely practiced hospitality than my mother. She would go all out. The table would be set with her own hand-painted dishes atop a cutwork linen cloth which she had made by hand (I now own one which took her seventeen years to complete), and each guest would have a place card of Mother's design and craftsmanship. All details in order. And . . . the meal, of course, her masterpiece.

She loved beauty. She was the first person, in fact, from whom I learned to look for and appreciate beauty—in nature, in art, in music, in colors. She constantly encouraged me to create something beautiful with my hands: my school notebooks, a table setting, my clothes closet, a flower arrangement, my attire. Something, *all* the time. I didn't always obey, but she always encouraged. And there was no moderation to her own areas of creativity and experimentation. The day before she died she had been to an oil painting class, a new medium (for her) which she had taken up about a year before. During that year she painted every day, and talked to me about it constantly—what joy it brought her, all the new techniques she was learning, how she wanted to improve, the idea of building her own frames, etc.

I vividly recall, as a young girl, being quickly bored with some domestic or school assignment and saying to her, "What can I do as soon as I finish this, Mama? Tell me something to do." And invariably her two words were, "Make something." I rarely remember her suggesting that I read or write or play ball. It was always, "Make something with your hands." Frequently she would suggest what I could make. Maybe she did that to save her own sanity, for occasionally (since I loved to sing), I would take the hymn book, march up to where she was sewing or cooking, and announce, "I'm going to sing every verse of every song in this book," and begin at verse one, page one. A few sessions of those renditions and one automatically responds, "Make something with your hands." At least that way all's quiet on the Texas front.

I suppose the best and most vivid memory I have of Mother is of the times she was studying her Bible. She would sit on her bed or at the dining table and read for hours. If she was not reading or making notes in her already well-marked Bible, her eyes would be closed in prayer or meditation. This was a common sight in our household, and that recollection of her, with all its positive attributes, is as engraved in my mind as the negative picture I spoke of earlier, when she slammed the door in a pout. The two pictures stand side by side.

But as much as Mother loved the scriptures and diligently sought to live by them, she was in her late fifties before they seemed to control her life to a greater degree than her moods, at least outwardly. The flesh, it seems, never wants to give up its wearying battle for control, does it? We read, we study, we memorize, we put scripture memory cards in every room in the house, and we maintain an active prayer life, but the battle goes on. This appeared to be the case certainly with Mother. Occasionally she would tell me of her private struggles and how much she wanted to grow up and let go of her own will and how hard it was; how she foundered in discouragement. But she held on, claiming promises, asking God for direction, and believing that He would one day indeed command her undivided attention. She unreservedly believed 2 Timothy 3:16-17, which reads:

> The whole Bible was given to us by inspiration from God and is useful to teach us what is true and to make us realize what is wrong in our lives; it straightens us out and helps us do what is right. It is God's way of making us well prepared at every point, fully equipped to do good to everyone.

For some reason I find all of this so hard to write. Perhaps it's because as Christians we are taught from childhood to honor our parents, giving them not only complete respect, but allegiance and loyalty. That means we don't have negative thoughts or feelings about them, or if we do, we seek to confess those thoughts immediately to God, thus clearing the air and cleansing our hearts from the sin of animosity. In this chapter, I have written things about my mother that I've never put on paper before: her moodiness, her inflexibility, her narrow viewpoint, her forcefulness in demanding I be like her. Information like that is hard to write, especially when I know it will be in print one day to be read by others who knew her and loved her. It gives me the distinct feeling also that I am being disloyal to the family name—something that was absolutely forbidden by my father. It brings to mind certain teachings that were mine in childhood, and it produces in me the feeling, "What will people think of your mother if you openly confess that?" And most assuredly, "What will they think of you?" But I also believe if these were the only facts about Mother that loomed up in my remembrance of her, perhaps there would be just cause to leave them unsaid, undisclosed. That is not the case.

An additional reason for my writing difficulty is that the dichotomy of any personality is always difficult to express. We want to think only the best of people. If we think the best, they will like us and we will like them and there will be no waves made by lack of unity. Especially in a family, and most especially in a Christian family. I have had Christian individuals say to me, "If you only knew how my mother *really* was, you wouldn't hold her in such high esteem." Or "My parents left a lot to be desired when it came to rearing me. They made one mistake after another and I'm sure I would be vastly different now were it not for their lack of knowledge in child raising." Maybe I feel I am doing that here by being so open about Mother. Transparency among Christians is dangerous at times, even though the Bible encourages it, because to stick our neck out means we run a very real chance of having it severed from our body by a legalistic believer who is running loose with his or her own axe to grind. Pardon me, I'm deviating from my point.

So here's the point: Now that I am a fifty-year-old woman looking back upon my life as affected by my family, I see that my mother taught me some extremely basic truths about life that no one else in my formative years could possibly have exhibited as clearly or as strongly as she—simply because of the exacting and very real contrasts in her nature. These mixtures of moods, attitudes, convictions, which appeared to be in conflict with one another in her person—dealing me such misery and heartache as a youngster—turned out to be the very ingredients that constitute the strength of my admiration for her today. I have learned that, more often than not, it is the frivolous, shallow, superficial individual who is the same predictable person all the time. Anyone with character or interest or depth invariably will have a soul that is marked by dualism—aspects of his or her personality that are inexplicable. The *really* unfortunate facet of this whole thing is that I was too young to perceive such a concept as an adolescent, when the knowledge of it would have benefited me greatly, and my mother was gone by the time my mind unlocked the value of this revelation.

Mother laughed as strongly as she cried, feared as deeply as she trusted, gave as easily as she withheld. Every expression of one emotion was the flip side of its counterpart. Naturally, conditions surrounding a fragile person of this type could be filled with tension, to say the least, and quite often they were. But life was never dull, even in its quietest moments.

So what is the reason for this rather academic discourse? Before I answer that with what I think is the key to Mother's life, both as it affected me and as it resulted in her own maturity, please read these verses from the book of Hebrews:

> For whatever God says to us is full of living power: it is sharper than the sharpest dagger, cutting swift and deep into our innermost thoughts and desires with all their parts, exposing us for what we really are. He knows about everyone, everywhere. Everything about us is bare and wide open to the all-seeing eyes of our living God; nothing can be hidden from him to whom we must explain all that we have done.

> But Jesus the Son of God is our great High Priest who has gone to heaven itself to help us; therefore let us never stop trusting him. This High Priest of ours understands our weaknesses, since he had the same temptations we do, though he never once gave way to them and sinned. So let us come boldly to the very throne of God and stay there to receive his mercy and to find grace to help us in our times of need (Hebrews 4:12-16).

See those words, ". . . exposing us for what we really are," in verse 12? In the King James Version (the edition from which Mother read and studied), that phrase reads, "is a discerner of the thoughts and intents of the heart."

Now here's what I believe to be the most important key to Mother's life, so if you're still with me, listen up. What I want to say is encompassed by that little word "intents." "Intent" means to be firmly directed or intense; having in mind a resolved motivation. As I envision Mother's perception of me, I am convinced that there was much she didn't or couldn't understand, due to the differences in our basic dispositions. Consequently, we often disagreed either verbally or in our hearts. She pouted, I anguished, and nothing was resolved. But . . . I am equally as convinced that her intentions for me were good. Right. Loving. It was our contrasting temperaments which got in the way of resolution, not simply Mother's wanting me to be like her and my inability to be so. That's it! And our temperaments were not the important issue, after all, that I thought they were for years. Our basic, honest intentions were the important motivators, but they couldn't be seen or felt because of the overriding characteristics of our individual differences. What a shame. Not only for me and Mother, but for anyone who finds him or herself in that predicament, and I venture to say there are many people who do. How often we are critical of other people because of our own inability to understand them, to perceive their intentions. Experience in dealing with people helps, of course, in reaching human understanding, but it is never the discerner that the Word of God is. It's the Bible and the application of scripture that teaches us about other people as well as ourselves. It is the sword that cuts into and exposes our thoughts.

In closing, let me consider for a few moments Mother's maturity in her twilight years. This is much easier to define. During Mother's days while we children were growing up, all her desires regarding child rearing were highly conscientious: that we grow in a knowledge of scripture, that we live and operate in truth, that we learn foundational habits to insure constructive futures, that we give proper respect to authority—the same desires any loving, attentive mother has for her children. To that end, she lived the major portion of her life, giving little thought to her own self-actualization. I believe God honored that commitment during her lifetime. He also honored her trust in Him. As those verses in Hebrews tell us, He understood her weaknesses, and I am certain she boldly approached His throne of grace on countless occasions (no doubt many times on my behalf). She remained there until He gave her His peace and His grace to help her in times of need. In fact, maybe that's what she was doing behind closed doors, instead of pouting . . . talking to God.

When I was about sixteen or seventeen, during those early days when one begins one's own search for identity, I saw Mother reading her Bible one day and I asked her, "Do you believe all that stuff, Mother?" She raised her head and looked at me quizzically for a moment. Then she smiled. "With all my heart," she said quietly. I can still see that smile and hear those words. That's the third mental picture in my mind's private gallery.

God took her through many years of giving up her own ways and dreams and she learned through disappointments to courageously say yes to Him. He mellowed her heart. He tempered her spirit. Then He took her home.

Edna St. Vincent Millay wrote:

The courage that my mother had
Went with her, and is with her still:
Rock from New England quarried;
Now granite in a granite hill.

The golden brooch my mother wore
She left behind for me to wear;
I have no thing I treasure more:
Yet, it is something I could spare.

Oh, if instead she'd left to me
The thing she took into the grave!—
That courage like a rock, which she
Has no more need of, and I have.[1]

I understand fully what Millay is saying. I, too, would love to have the rock-like courage my mother took away with her. There are many times when I feel my own is not enough. But she left me something else, something even better: my first exposure to God's word, which I too believe now . . . with all my heart. Mother used to say to me,

Yes, our natural lives will fade as grass does when it becomes all brown and dry. All our greatness is like a

1. Edna St. Vincent Millay, *Collected Poems*, ed. Norma Millay (New York: Harper & Row, 1956), p. 459.

flower that droops and falls; but the Word of the Lord will last forever. And his message is the Good News that was preached to you.

Those words are from 1 Peter.

MY OLDER BROTHER

It is our duty to set ourselves an end beyond our individual concerns, beyond our convenient, agreeable habits, higher than our own selves, and disdaining laughter, hunger, even death, to toil night and day to attain that end. No, not to attain it. The self-respecting soul, as soon as he reaches his goal, places it still further away. Not to attain it, but never to halt in the ascent. Only thus does life acquire nobility and oneness.

You've already met my older brother, Orville Swindoll. He wrote the foreword to this book, which, if you started at the beginning, you've read. Well, maybe you've not actually "met" him, but you are at least acquainted with one of his many talents: his writing ability. I have wondered, at times, if Orville were born with a pen and paper in hand. Listen to this brief note he composed (and typed) at age ten, which I found in that old cedar chest.

Dear Cousins:

For the last week I have been begging Dad to let me write you a letter on the typewriter and this is the first time he has agreed.

Today is very pretty, the sun is shining brightly and it is almost like Spring. Since I got a red wagon for Christmas I have to have pretty weather so I can play outside. Sister and Charles both like to ride in my new wagon and trailer and we all three have a big time together. I want to thank you both for the nice things you sent us for Christmas. I surely needed the brush set and it will last me a long time. Sister surely has lots of fun reading the little books and even Charles has learned to read two of the books through. He still has his airplane and gets lots of fun playing with it.

Mother is writing a letter to you also, so I will not write any more at this time.

Write to us again soon and come down to see us sometime. Bye bye—

Lovingly,
Orville Earl

By the time he was fourteen he had graduated to the level of poetry. This was written to Mother on her birthday in 1945 when she became thirty-eight:

Through fourteen years of happiness
I've known no greater bliss,
Than to call you 'Mother'
You're the one I'd most miss.

Through all my little troubles,
And all my fears, though slight,
I can only say, 'dear Mother,
You've helped with all your might.'

You've been so kind, so gentle.
I could never hope for more
And until my wife comes, I'll always say,
'You're the one I adore.'

Your ever-loving son,
Orville

Admittedly that could use a little editing, and it is a tad saccharine, but at least it's very creative and I'm sure my mother cherished it. After all, she had saved it all those years. (My birthday card the same year probably said something unimaginative, like "When do we cut the cake?")

But Orville advanced in his writing style and abilities. The following piece of prose was extracted from another birthday greeting to mother, a lengthy letter written sixteen years later. I would like to quote it all, as it is a beautiful reflection of one who seemed to be without enough words to adequately express the love and appreciation he felt, but I'll not take the time and space. Here are the closing paragraphs:

> It is most comforting to me to know that as you grow older, the faith you taught us as children is your own bulwark and high tower, giving you strength and assurance in the passing months and years. I rejoice too in the physical health and blessing you enjoy, and pray that your remaining years shall be crowned with such continually.
>
> As my own responsibilities as a parent multiply, and now finding myself the proud father of three precious children, I feel I am coming to better understand the joys *and* the heartaches that you experienced in manifold measure in raising your three. And I so often find myself repeating to my own the very words and exhortations which I frequently heard in my youth—evidence of your faithfulness in instilling strong Godly principles for life into us.
>
> All this is in tribute to you, Mom, from a son who loves you with all his heart. I am confident I could fill volumes with memories of your many virtues, but I confess that one of them stands out to me more prominently than all the rest, and I think it did more to shape my life than almost anything else. I trust it has become a central part of me, and a characteristic expression of my life—especially to my own children. That virtue to me is—tender love, unbounding love, merciful love—love that God undoubtedly put into your heart as a mother. I seem to have needed an unusually large portion of it, and your response was unabating. My reciprocation to such selfless love certainly has been no equal; but I shall thank the Lord—and you—if one day my children can say something similar about me. In such case I know where the credit

belongs, and from whence the virtue sprang forth.

May this year for you be crowned with infinite blessings from our Lord—who so loved . . . He gave.

Your own,
Orville Earl

Orville has now written and published three books, and he told
me the last time we spoke on the telephone (about a month ago)
he had ten more in his head that he wanted to write.

Everybody should be reared in a household with an older
brother like Orville. It is truly an education in itself, apart from
all other forms of learning.

In looking back now, I view him as a child with a tremendously high IQ, a bit of a genius, who wanted to accomplish more
by the age of eighteen, let's say, than any other human being
who ever lived. But at that vantage point, he was a pain in the
neck! Being the oldest child in the family, he had a tendency to
inform his younger sister (myself) and younger brother (Chuck)
that he ruled the roost. He wasn't really a bully, as you might
think, because he had a loving temperament. He was just hard-
headed. Couple that with his extremely fast perception of all
phenomena and his desire to accomplish heights unknown to
children, and you've got Trouble—Right Here In River City.
Chuck and I, not being exactly taciturn in our own behaviors, re-
belled at his lordly ways and, naturally, sparks flew a great deal of
the time. Or if it was too quiet, my mother would suspect Orville
was up to something and would say to me, "Go see what Orville
Earl is doing and tell him to stop it, whatever it is." Even suspi-
cion ran high when Orville was anywhere on the premises, and
there was generally good reason. Let me give you a little background:

Because I don't recall the exact chronological progression
of these events, I'll lump them together to give you an overall picture of what happened at our house, as well as to attempt to
show you a trend which indicated Orville was destined to nobility (at least in my thinking) in several realms. To provide a time
frame as a springboard for your thoughts, let's say these various

episodes occurred in Orville's life (and consequently in our family's life as well) within a six or seven year period, from the time he was fifteen until he was twenty or twenty-one. I was thirteen months younger than he and Chuck was two years younger than I. So there we were, the three Swindoll kids, all growing up together in a small Christian home in Houston, Texas. You've got the scene, OK?

I should begin by saying that Orville has *always* loved music, and every other pursuit, even in its deepest intensity, never vanquished that love. My parents told me that when Orville was a very small boy, he would cry if the music on the radio was "too beautiful," asking them to shut it off. So quite early in life, because of this natural inclination toward music, he wanted to study piano. Our house, cacophonous as it was anyway with the tireless jabber of three kids all talking at once and the corrective expletives of two parents, had added to it daily the monotony of do-re-mi-fa-sol-la-ti-do from the piano keys. Orville was faithful in his practice. He would sit at the piano for hours at a stretch while my younger brother and I ran in and out of the house, getting the football or catcher's mitt, our rubber guns, paint sets, fishing poles, or whatever we needed for one of our many outdoor escapades. Orville's musical aspirations and skills grew with each passing year. I recall his announcement one night at the dinner table (where all of us discussed family issues at length) that he had every intention of being a concert pianist and composer. Of course we all took him seriously, since that seemed an appropriate ambition for one who sat at the piano most of his free time anyway. However, shortly after this dinner-time disclosure, I noticed he became more and more interested in science.

Being bright anyway, Orville had little trouble with academics in general—he brought home books from school, pored over them with great conscientiousness, and more often than not turned in A papers and did exceedingly well on tests. He read rapidly and the family soon became aware that not only was he reading his school books on science, but library books, and journals and magazines on medicine. Somewhere, somehow, he managed to persuade Mother that he needed rabbits and guinea pigs in order to learn their habits and anatomy and to perform certain medical experiments on them, so she consented. Before long, our backyard had its own small animal farm from which Orville drew his specimens for needed experiments or dissection. I'll always remember the afternoon I walked into the boys' bedroom after school, only to see the body of an innocent victim—a guinea pig, dissected, on top of a drafting board sitting on their study desk. The parts of the poor baby were all lying to the left of the body, in perfect order, with identifying labels under each organ. To the right lay an open library book entitled *Animal Structures.* I expressed my horror to Mother, asking her what Orville had done to "Sam," the guinea pig, and she reported, as her eyes rolled from left to right, "Well, how can I be a doctor if I don't know what's inside things?" She was quoting Orville's earlier words to her. He now sat at the piano, doing Czerny exercises.

The most outstanding incident of this "medical era," however, was a comical circumstance that involved my father as much as Orville. In the hopes of entering a science fair at school during that particular year, Orville decided to purchase male and female fruitflies, *Drosophila melanogaster.* He wanted to raise them and study their mating habits . . . a subject that often became the topic of dinner conversation. I'm sure Orville hoped to parlay his findings into scientific fame.

Because fruitflies are such tiny things, they had to be kept in a small container and raised in a gelatinous culture, called agar-agar. This container then had to "live" in a cold environment. Orville determined the best and healthiest habitat for his newly-purchased *Drosophila* would be the refrigerator. Therefore, he put the agar-agar and flies into a milk bottle under a tight lid and proceeded to keep a watchful eye on them every time the refrigerator door opened. I must admit, it was interesting to watch them, learn about their habits from my studious and informed brother, and realize they were indeed multiplying right there next to the grape jelly and cheddar cheese.

The only problem was the agar-agar. Being made from seaweed, it looked much like milk in a thickened state. Since the flies lived in a milk bottle, one had to be very careful not to mistake one jar for the other. Of course we had all been verbally warned as well as reminded with notes of caution in and on the refrigerator. However, my father during this year worked swing shift and it was his nightly habit to have a bowl of cereal after he got home, before retiring. The fateful night came when Orville was about two-thirds through with his experiment, and Daddy, in his tired state, grabbed the wrong bottle. He took the lid off and began to pour, only to realize nothing was coming out because agar-agar is so thick. Nothing, that is, except those precious fruitflies. My dad was horrified, awakened Orville, and the two of them conducted a midnight search for those miniscule flies. I can still hear Orville whispering, "Look for the males, Daddy, they're the more colorful." Of course, it was too late then, and that ambitious experiment ended in Daddy's repeated apologies to Orville and his own regret for lack of closure. But life moves on.

Hypnosis was the next great adventure. As the library books on medicine were returned and the science fair was behind us, Orville replaced this phase with a desire to learn hypnotism. Of course, since the family members were all Christian, this new adventure, while often being associated with the occult, was on an amateur level only and kept under the watchful eyes of my parents. I think they knew it would pass eventually, given enough time, but not before Orville hypnotized, or at least attempted hypnosis, on both Chuck and me. Under the spell of Orville's fledgling ability, we fetched various items of his bidding, such as the evening paper from the yard, the car keys for Mother, and his school books, all the while surreptitiously winking at one another in clear assurance that this was done for show only, so that our older brother would be satisfied with his accomplishment and move on to other things. This state of development was rather short-lived, actually, and we later confessed to Orville that we had feigned hypnotic states. I don't believe his disappointment was too great, because in no time he was taking pictures, developing his own film, and asking hundreds of questions at the local photo shop about the difficulties involved in building one's own camera.

The family bathroom (also the only bathroom) became Orville's darkroom. And even though the homemade camera never came into being, many well-developed pictures did, but all at the expense of various irate family members who insisted our need for the darkroom was greater than his.

Because I want to move on in this marathon of events, I won't go into detail about his adventures in dog raising and breeding, including a five-year subscription to *Dog World* magazine, or ham radio operating with all of its interesting sideline developments, or his in-depth study of mathematics, electronics, chemistry, or physics. Each of these disciplines held Orville's utmost interest as he studied it, worked through its related problems, deleted seemingly irrelevant data, and obtained a workable and useable grasp of all the essential elements. The exciting aspect of all of it is that each of these areas still holds his interest.

Even though there were many things about Orville's personality and behavior as a child that I found insufferable, there were other significant intangible qualities that I admired and do admire to this day: his sold-out dedication to a task, his ambitious dreams, his desire to excel, his love of quality, his amazing sense of organization, his fearlessness in attempting new quests, his ability to see the fun and challenge of the unknown. And it's interesting that all of these characteristics which began in the seed-bed of our childhood circus-times are the intangibles I now seek in my own life. With Orville, it seemed, no two days were the same. His life was filled with excitement and adventure as he avidly pursued knowledge. And he did it all with such fervor and joy.

It has been said that "the trouble with life is that it is so daily." That's very true. But coupled with that truth is the fact that life is generally what we make it. If we are not content with the sameness or "daily-ness" of living, then we're going to set about to change it. My first exposure to this philosophy came from my older brother. He never said that to me in words, but I saw it repeatedly in his life. As he reached one goal it only meant the setting of a new one, still further away. And he has never halted in that ascent.

Orville is a missionary/pastor in Argentina. He has lived and worked there for the past twenty-three years. His wonderful, loving, patient wife, as well as their four grown children, are bilingual, musical, relational, and adventuresome. To them, Buenos Aires is home. Orville built his own home there about four years ago and he is spending his life doing what he now loves more than anything else in the world: introducing people to Jesus Christ, loving them, and discipling them in the faith.

Several years ago, he and I were visiting face to face, reminiscing about old times and laughing about those countless endeavors of his as a youngster. I asked him if he would do anything differently if he had those years to do over. He said, "Sis, the only thing I would do differently is to learn more. I would have read more books, learned more of the academics, tried more experiments, built more radios, studied other languages, attended more concerts, spent more time in getting to know people. There never is enough time to learn it all, and if you want to be effective in any realm, you can't know too much. I'm not sorry for one single thing I delved into as a kid, because at one time or another, as a missionary or a pastor, I've used it all. Well, all except maybe hypnosis." We both laughed.

I'm not sure exactly when Orville decided to go into the ministry and become a missionary, but that date doesn't matter. When he was about twenty he did a tour of duty in the Navy, and I feel sure that it was during those days God called Orville to his highest duty, that is, to give completely his time, energy, talents, and life to the Lord Jesus Christ. When Orville came home from that stint he had changed somehow. He seemed quieter, deeper, sweeter, and more resolved. It was as though his inner eye were set like flint. When he told the family of his desire to enter the ministry, each one of us knew he meant serious business. He diligently and constantly investigated the scriptures and was in earnest about every thought and activity in his life, matching the excellence of this high calling. He pursued his new resolution with the same firmness of purpose he had shown in all previous undertakings.

Two of my most vivid recollections of Orville's seriousness during those days are his enjoyment of singing hymns as he accompanied himself at the piano, and his faithfulness in prayer at bedtime. If he had been out in the evening on a date or to a meeting or a social function, he never went to bed without kneeling down and spending time in prayer. One night it was quite late when Orville came home. The rest of the family was already in bed. He quietly tiptoed down the hallway, passed the door of my bedroom, and went into his room. I was awake and heard him walk by. After about ten minutes of quietness, I heard his clear bass voice singing in the darkness:

> And can it be that I should gain
> An interest in the Savior's blood?
> Died He for me, who caused His pain?
> For me, who Him to death pursued?
> Amazing love! How can it be that Thou,
> my God, shouldst die for me?

It was beautiful. Such rich tones even in all their tranquility and softness. I loved it. I lay there in bed, listening to Orville's singing and to the words of that magnificent old hymn.

And for the first time, I was truly hypnotized.

MY YOUNGER BROTHER

That part of Christ's nature which was profoundly human helps us to understand Him and love Him and to pursue His Passion as though it were our own. If He had not within Him this warm human element, He would never be able to touch our hearts with such assurance and tenderness; He would not be able to become a model for our lives.
We struggle, we see Him struggle also, and we find strength. We see that we are not alone in the world; He is fighting at our side . . . we have a model in front of us now, a model who opens the way for us and gives us strength.

When one comes from a family such as mine—three children all reared in the same environment, two boys and one girl, with each of the boys not only becoming ministers, but prominent and successful by the world's standards—many questions are asked. At least, *I* am asked questions frequently. Things like:

What was your family *really* like when you were growing up?
Which brother decided to go into the ministry first?
Was your father a minister? (A very common question.)
Did you ever consider the ministry, too?
How do your brothers differ in their personalities and preaching styles?
When all of you are together, do you talk about

theological issues?

How did your parents feel about their two sons pursuing spiritual callings and their daughter pursuing a secular career?

Does God bless your career to the same degree as their callings?

(I was honestly asked that last question once, if you can believe it, but I thought I answered it well. I said, "Yes, She does," and went right on!)

It has been my experience that any time we are with or know of individuals who have achieved recognition in this life or have touched others in such a way that lives are changed, we are curious as to what makes them tick . . . humanly speaking, I mean. That is a natural query. Of course, those of us who, having personally put our faith and trust in the claims of Jesus Christ, are in the kingdom of God and know something of the teachings of the Bible realize that it is the Holy Spirit's enablement alone that actually transforms lives. I'm not talking about that (remember, I'm not the preacher!). I'm talking about human qualities that God has given us which we call our makeup or our temperament. I, for one, am very interested in people's temperaments, because their behavior is a reflection of their temperament. Knowing more about people's natures helps me understand them to a greater degree, and it permits me to appreciate what they have overcome in order to get where they are in life. Additionally, it encourages me to know myself better and to seek higher levels of achievement in my own life.

I'm not telling you anything new—anything you don't already know. The only reason I reiterate it here is to say that I understand why people ask those questions. I ask them, too, about others, and the reason I don't ask them in this case is that I already know the answers, since we're talking about my family.

When we were children, I thought every home was like ours. Or, to be more accurate, I never thought about it at all. It never occurred to me that our training or our parents' supervision was any different—more strict or less strict, more loving or less loving—than in any other home. To me, we were the Swindoll family, living our lives in the normal way of living. At that time it didn't enter my mind that my brothers might be in the ministry one day or that they would be dealing with the joys or problems that a life of high visibility produces. In a way, my thoughts were like those of Leonard Bernstein's father, who once said of his son, "How was I to know he was going to grow up to be Leonard Bernstein?" One doesn't think of those particular issues when one is "in" them, and I don't believe we contemplate subjects of that magnitude as children. Or if we do, we don't fully understand what we're thinking at the time. It's only in retrospect that we can comprehend what qualities of life were woven into our fiber.

It wasn't until I was grown, therefore, that I realized each one of us viewed our respective childhoods differently; not only differently with respect to what they were like, but differently from each other.

In a conversation I had with Orville after we were both adults, he referred to our exemplary home life as children, painting one word picture after another about Mother and Daddy being model, attentive parents. I remember distinctly his using the word "exemplary"—an almost idealistic view of childhood. And in many ways our home life was exemplary in that our parents emphasized respect for authority, morality, allegiance to the family, principles of good conduct, academics, the importance of the arts, and above all the teachings of scripture. But when he said that, I recall thinking, ". . . exemplary? Yeah, well maybe it was after all. That's funny, I sort of thought it was like everybody else's family—average, everyday living."

Then what came as even more of a revelation to me was a sermon I heard my younger brother, Charles Swindoll, preach several years ago on the family, in which he referred to his nucleus family, confessing that he felt much like an "afterthought" as a child. I heard him make reference to the fact that when he was born, his home already had a completed family circle—a father, a mother, a son, a daughter—and that he never felt he quite fit in anywhere. That was the first time I ever considered such a thing: the possibility that one of us had actually felt left out. But now I can see how his feelings must have been accurate in that. Envisioning my older brother's closeness to Mother and my own closeness to Daddy, where did that leave Chuck? Naturally, with the view that he was indeed an afterthought.

What a striking disclosure that was to me, because it enabled me to recognize how differently we all viewed the same circumstance and how correct each one of us was in his or her own perceptions. It almost puts reality in the eye of the beholder, and it most assuredly affects how we face life. At least in my younger brother's case it was the embryo of thoughts and feelings that contained all the rudiments necessary for God to start making Himself known, available, trustworthy, and utterly constant. I believe it was in this seed-bed context that God first began His ultimate design and purpose for Chuck's life—in the very fact that one of Chuck's earliest feelings was that he felt unwanted by his parents. Let me be more definitive.

As a catapult for our considerations, let's look for a moment at four verses from an excellent poem, written by William Cowper. It's called *Providence.*

> God moves in a mysterious way
> His wonders to perform:
> He plants his footsteps in the sea,
> And rides upon the storm.
>
> Deep in unfathomable mines
> Of never-failing skill
> He treasures up his bright designs,
> And works his sovereign will.
>
> His purposes will ripen fast,
> Unfolding every hour;
> The bud may have a bitter taste
> But sweet will be the flower.
>
> Blind unbelief is sure to err,
> And scan his work in vain;
> God is His own interpreter
> And He will make it plain.

That poem sets the perfect intangible stage for the chain of events that I am about to relate.

It is improbable that you who hold this book in your hands have not at least heard of Chuck Swindoll. Chuck is, in my opinion, the finest Bible teacher in America today. He is bright, knowledgeable, practical, creative, balanced, warm, and extremely witty—a rare combination of superlative gifts in all categories, blended together in a vessel that God has chosen to use mightily in His work. Now, you're probably thinking, "Of course Luci would say that. She's biased because he's her brother." And you are right. I am biased because we are not only bound together in spiritual unity, but in family unity as well. I happen to know, too, that I am Chuck's favorite sister, a fact in which I take great comfort, you understand, considering his wide range of choices.

Among the numerous questions posed to me nowadays is "How does it feel to be Chuck Swindoll's sister?" And while I think that is a rather trivial query, I realize, once again, why people ask it. And I'll answer it here for all the world to see. It feels great! I love Chuck. I am inordinately proud of his many accomplishments, especially in light of what seemed to be a major handicap he experienced as a child. Although you would not believe it now, when Chuck was a boy, he stuttered so badly we often could not understand what he was trying to say. I remember once, at the evening dinner table, he asked for something to be passed to him—the mashed potatoes, or the vegetables, I forget—and by the time we understood him, someone else had eaten the food he wanted. It sounds funny now, but then it was serious. Since those days I have read that stuttering is often the result of insecurity, and now that I know his feelings of being unloved and unwanted as a child, I am sure that was the reason for his stuttering, at least in part. But he didn't just grow out of it. He consciously set about to change it, even as a boy. He seemed to employ a method.

Some of my earliest recollections of Chuck are of his quoting poetry. He loved poetry (still does), and early in his life he began memorizing it as well as quoting it to any of us who would listen. With his quick mind, he grasped the words easily; then he would slowly launch into a program of poetry for Mother or me or any captive audience, trying to say each word carefully to avoid stuttering. Gradually his speech improved, as did his memory bank I am sure. By the time he entered high school, Chuck was intensely interested in drama and theater. He and his teacher, Richard Niemi, worked diligently together to strengthen Chuck's speaking and acting abilities . . . so much so that his stuttering disappeared altogether and he seriously considered, for a time, a career in acting. (I have found myself wondering if Mr. Niemi is still alive and is aware of Chuck's ministry.)

In addition to Chuck's interest in drama, my parents wanted each of us to study a musical instrument. Chuck chose the clarinet. Since he also loved football and wanted to attend the high school games, the clarinet permitted him an opportunity to perform in the school band and go to the games, too. Initially Mother and Dad encouraged him to take piano lessons (perhaps "coerced" is a better word than "encouraged"), but after a short term of that, it was as though he had his own dreams about musical pursuits and insisted on the clarinet. Even though Daddy referred to Chuck's clarinet as a "machine," with Chuck's constant rebuttal, "Daddy, it's not a machine; it's an instrument"—the choice of clarinet won out over the piano, and off he went to the weekly ball games, instrument in hand.

Before long, not only was he becoming proficient on the clarinet, playing with more beauty and agility all the time, but he was studying oboe and saxophone as well. And he was making his own reeds for each of those instruments. One afternoon he brought home from school a flute. After an hour or so of practice on that, interspersed with Orville's nightly piano virtuosity, Chuck announced at dinner that he was going to start playing the flute in the school band, to which Daddy said, "What about your machine?"

"Instrument," Chuck said. "Oh, I'm going to play that, too. I want to play more than one instrument, Daddy, and all these are easy to take to the games. Besides, Mr. Seastrand (he was our marvelously talented high school music teacher) needs people who can play several instruments 'cause people are always dropping out of band. So I'm going to study the flute."

Forsooth! No lights flashed. No bells went off. Chuck had simply once again decided he was going to master a skill, and with dogged determination he set out to achieve his goal. When he graduated from high school, he won a much deserved drama award and was skilled on the clarinet, oboe, saxophone, flute, and piccolo.

Several years later on the island of Okinawa, while Chuck was serving as a member of the Third Division, U. S. Marine Corps Band, he had the honor of playing clarinet for the Emperor of Japan—an occasion he says he will never forget. Daddy called me after he had received a letter from his son. "Guess what?" he said. "Charles got to play his machine for the Emperor of Japan." We were both thrilled. However, I couldn't help correcting Daddy in Chuck's defense, "Instrument, Daddy. Instrument."

At the time Chuck joined the Marine Corps, he had seriously begun to consider the possibility of entering the ministry. Truthfully, I'm sure he felt the strict discipline of the military service and his time away from all his loved ones would give him the environment needed for God to clearly bring his considerations into focus and clarify any doubts. He had spent his time after high school pursuing a trade, diligently studying the Bible, and actively engaging in various aspects of church activity: music, witnessing, evangelistic preaching, etc. But perhaps he felt in limbo with respect to a definite calling or career. Maybe he needed that final disciplinary punch that only a drill sergeant can engender. And he got it!

The family benefited also, in a unique way, from Chuck's time away from home. We received his letters—and there were scores of them. Letters to his wife, his parents, his sister, his brother, his friends. I have kept all of those to me, and I have inherited those to his parents—what a chronicle of events and spiritual development they portray. I re-read them from time to time just for fun, or if I'm feeling blue. And I never fail to find encouragement. Here's an example, from a letter dated May 4, 1958, written in Okinawa. He was responding to the fact that I had lost my job in a small company where I had been employed:

Dear "Sweets,"

Upon receiving Dad's last letter, I read of your position being terminated at the Exploration Company. Sis, dear, God has something greater for you. I have never seen it fail—God always puts us in the roughest situations at the strangest times. He delights in moving believers into new situations without even cluing us in on it. Whenever we become an effective witness by means of growth in the Word, God begins immediately putting us to the real test—that long, hard climb toward maturity. Remember, dear one, God continues to provide even among the tests He places us under. You are now well on your way—Suffering.

I'm sure you remember how we used to speak so often of how greatly we desired maturity. Well, you are finding out more each day just what "maturity" really means . . . He always knocks from under us any crutch, leaning post, or anything else that might tend to take our eyes off the Lord.

May I assure you of the prayers of your loving brother, who is too far away to be with you and visit you during these times of waiting and trusting, but knows very well the full impact of believing prayers.

While Chuck was on the island of Okinawa, his memory work and Bible study time multiplied a hundredfold. He set to memory literally hundreds of verses, hymns, and poems. He tells an amusing account of attending an open air evangelistic meeting one night when the director held up a twenty-dollar bill, offering it to the individual who could accurately quote the Ten Commandments. Unfortunately, Chuck had not memorized that particular passage from Exodus 20, but with such an incentive, he went straight to the barracks after the meeting and learned it. He told me later that since that accomplishment not one living soul has offered him twenty dollars for the Ten Commandments. "But I'm ready in case they do," he added.

Chuck taught a small Bible class to other men at Camp Courtney, his Marine base in Okinawa, for which he prepared as enthusiastically as he does now for his nationwide ministry. Although he was disappointed at the time he wrote this letter in June of 1958, you'll find these words almost laughable in light of the way God has blessed Chuck's commitment to the scriptures:

> My Bible classes are such a blessing to each one of us because we all enjoy digging into the Word of Grace. The teacher has much to learn but the students are quite patient with him. There are four men who are consistently faithful to the class and a couple of "visitors," off and on. Last Thursday, no one came (except me), so I just spent the time in study and prayer. It does take faith and patience to continue without visible improvement, but I know Isaiah 55:10 and 11 still hold true. To plan an hour and a half of Bible exposition and study, then have no one come doesn't discourage me however. It challenges me all the more to trust the Lord for the victory. I usually spend around 15-20 hours of preparation before my weekly class and if no one else learns anything, *I* certainly do.

I must agree. He certainly did. Chuck entered Dallas Theological Seminary in the fall of 1959 and graduated magna cum laude in May, 1963. Out of the forty-four different classes he took during that four year period, he made only two grades below an A, and they were B's. He had been there about a week when we chatted on the phone one day. I asked him how he thought he would like seminary. "Great!" was his reply. "Already, after one week of classes, I'm six months behind. This is going to be great. I'm going to love it." The following summer he took his first course in Hebrew, an extremely difficult class, I understand from those who live through it, and he even loved that. "The first test was so strange, Sis," he told me. "Didn't even look like a test. It looked like a rag rug."

When Chuck graduated from seminary, his thesis was entitled, "The Teaching Ministry of the Pastor/Teacher," and he was awarded three of the twelve awards given to the outstanding graduates:

The H. A. Ironside award in Expository Preaching

The Arthur C. Gannett award in Christian Education

The Faculty Award

Chuck's humor has seen him through some very low times, such as his first course in learning Hebrew. It's as though it's his catalyst for taking him out of the anguish and putting him into the challenge. I have observed that characteristic in his personality time and time again. About seven years ago at Christmas, I ran by his house—which is about a mile from mine—to drop off my Christmas gifts, and found everyone in the family was sick except Chuck. Every family member had the flu. I felt so sorry for him, having to care for various children and his wife in different stages of this debilitating virus. When I arrived, Chuck and his younger daughter, Colleen, were the only two who were up. Partially opened gifts were lying about, and Chuck was having a cup of coffee. He looked extremely tired, but he smiled and greeted me warmly, as always, inviting me to stay awhile. Colleen asked her father if she could open one of her gifts under the Christmas tree, and he said, "Sure, honey, if you feel like it." She chose an enormous box, about as tall as she was, and upon unwrapping it, discovered a doll that someone in the church had given her. The doll could do practically anything. It was a darling little girl with lots of moving parts.

Colleen seemed so thrilled and said, as she read the label on the box, "Oh, look, Daddy and Aunt Luci. This doll does it all: It walks, talks, wets, cries, eats . . ."

We joined in her happiness; then Chuck said very seriously, "Colleen, does it vomit? We can't have one more thing around here that vomits." I cracked up! And I thought, "How can he do it—be so funny when he is tired and everybody is sick? What a guy!"

Chuck's books and booklets are well known, with twenty-eight in print. His radio program, "Insight for Living," broadcasts daily over 400 stations and was selected as the most outstanding Christian ministry in radio broadcasting in America for the year 1982. And the list goes on.

I know him so well and generally I know how he thinks. I know his strengths and weaknesses. I am acquainted with some of the areas in which he struggles, and there are countless things about him I admire. But if I had to define his most salient quality, that part of his essence which receives my greatest admiration, it would be his absolute refusal to dwell on the negative. To camp on the struggle. He simply will not be defeated in his spirit. Oh, I've seen him low or depressed for a time, like all human beings, over things around him that appear to be falling apart. But before long he rises up like a phoenix out of a nest of ashes, soaring upward and flying to the heights, thinking of a dozen creative ways to take his eyes off the struggle. With that kind of spirit, the sky's the limit.

Like the rest of the Christian world, I watch Chuck, only my viewpoint is a bit different from yours. I have a panoramic advantage, to be sure, since I knew him from a family circle where he never felt he fit in, to forty-nine years later where seemingly the whole world cries out for his time. From a kid who stuttered to a man of verbal eloquence.

Just last week I had gotten up at 4:45 A.M. to take a brisk walk before going to work. I try to do that every morning to get the old bod moving and the kinks out. I had walked about a mile and was on my way home, hot and eager to sit down, when a block and a half ahead of me I spotted Chuck, jogging in the morning semi-darkness. He was really moving and there was no way for old, tired me to catch him. As I watched the back of that tilted head bob up and down, I thought, "Well, there he goes. Always ahead of the pack. At that rate, he's never going to gain back that fifty-three pounds he's lost. Gosh! I'll bet he's been up since 4:00, running all over this neighborhood. Where does he get the energy?" Then this scripture popped into my head:

> Forgetting the past and looking forward to what lies ahead, I strain to reach the end of the race and receive the prize for which God is calling us up to heaven because of what Christ Jesus did for us.

Even if our talents were exactly the same, the likelihood of my catching up with Chuck—in almost any race—is slim, whether that be dieting, jogging, playing an instrument, learning an ancient language, memorizing scripture, preaching to the whole of North America, writing books, or overcoming a childhood insecurity. But it's not necessarily because he's more proficient or better equipped than I am. We both have the same source of strength. It's because too often I look at the past and he looks at the prize. I dwell on the struggle and he dwells on the Savior. There will always be the negative, ready to defeat my spirit and hold me back. What I need to remember is that races are never won by looking back. They are won by the anticipation of what lies ahead. That makes all the difference.

MY FRIENDS

*A goodly number of pleasures have fallen my lot
in the course of a lifetime;
I have no reason to complain.*

Six years ago this summer, a hilarious event occurred in my life that I would like to recount for you. My dear and zany friend, Marilyn Meberg, and I were returning from a Christian Women's Club evening meeting where I had provided the music, when in casual conversation we began to chat about her next speaking engagement, which was to occur on a Saturday at a nearby restaurant. Since Marilyn is my favorite speaker among women and I always enjoy hearing what she has to say (knowing it will not only be encouraging and delivered well, but also spiced with humor), I asked if I might accompany her to the engagement, just to keep her company and to benefit once again from her speaking prowess. Marilyn objected, claiming that surely I would be bored because she planned to give a talk I had heard numerous times. She felt it would be a waste of my time on a Saturday.

We tossed around our different viewpoints on that subject, and we discussed some nutty ideas of my coming to the meeting in disguise or with a peculiarity that only she would know about . . . just for fun . . . just to see if I could pull it off . . . And all the while we were laughing heartily at the possible absurdities that could actually take place, were I brave enough.

Then suddenly, as we were turning into Marilyn's driveway so I could drop her off before coming home, she decided to put to me an actual challenge—one of the many mad and crazy ideas we had considered. (I don't know why she continues to do this, knowing full well that taking up ridiculous contests is one of my favorite forms of recreation.) Nevertheless, she outlined the format of her challenge, with a rich reward at the conclusion if I would agree. She said, "Luci, I will take you to the Hobbitt Restaurant as my guest, if you will do the following on Saturday at the women's luncheon where I'm speaking . . ."

Now, wait a minute! Before I tell you the requirements for my prize, let me acquaint you with the Hobbitt, a restaurant to which I had never been but had longed to go. The Hobbitt is an exceptional establishment in every sense of the word. It offers a one-sitting-per-evening, multi-course, set-price dining experience that has no equal in Southern California. Reservations are required literally months in advance. The evening begins promptly at 7:30 P.M., when the guests meet in the wine cellar for half an hour of hors d'oeuvres, champagne, and conversation. At eight o'clock everyone moves upstairs to the dining area for a seven-course dinner, interrupted halfway through to visit The Hobbitt Gallery, an exhibit of fine art. Every guest has the same menu which changes weekly and is rarely repeated. Men are to dress in coat and tie, women in long skirts. Very elegant!

Sound fun? Sound delicious? Sound unique? Well, my friends, it is all of that . . . and more. And to think, I could have it all without spending one red cent. But—and here's the catch—were I to fulfill Marilyn's demands, the payment for such an evening would cost me in self-respect. This was her proposal:

"Luci, you must come to the luncheon in a dress and dark glasses."

I thought, "All right! No problem."

"And Luci, you must stay at least thirty minutes."

Again, "No problem, Marilyn—thirty minutes out of a Saturday is a piece of cake . . . so what's the deal?"

Then, "You must wear your Mobil hardhat* and when spo-

---

*It should be noted here that I have been employed by Mobil Oil Corporation for a number of years, and my present job requires me to carry a hardhat in my car for times when I am called upon to appear at a scene where one might be needed.

ken to, respond with a speech impediment! And . . . you have to act totally unaware of your strange appearance . . . as though you feel perfectly at ease and at home dressed and speaking in that manner."

Needless to say, I had a fit! The Hobbitt, in all its succulent fantasy, seemed to sink into the regions of my mental never-never land as it was being replaced by the apparition of Luci Swindoll in dark glasses, dress, Mobil hardhat, looking normal while talking with a noticeable speech impediment at a luncheon for sedate, respectable Christian women. I couldn't do it. I simply could not consent to such terms, and no meal was worth the price of the utter destruction of my sense of dignity. Naturally, Marilyn was laughing uncontrollably, and I too joined in as I envisioned how truly funny that would be in such a setting. She got out of the car with one final dangling of the bait—"Remember. You've always wanted to eat at The Hobbitt. You'll never have a better offer." Then she closed the door and walked away.

When Saturday rolled around, I was recalling our idiotic bet as I went about doing my morning chores, when without the slightest provocation, a little voice inside my head said, "Do it."

I stopped dead in my tracks and out loud said, "What?"

"Do it, Luci. Don your hardhat and hit that meeting. Think of the fun you'd have . . . And Marilyn? Well, she'll drop her teeth. She's so wacky all the time, she's probably forgotten about the bet altogether. Imagine the look on her face when she sees you standing in that room, dressed as she prescribed, acting as though you belong there. She'll die. And . . . you'll be the winner—you can relive it over and over again for the rest of your life. Dinner at The Hobbitt! Do it!"

Taking that to be the voice of the Holy Spirit, I began to get dressed. By this time I was jazzed with the idea, and with my purpose in mind, I found I could hardly wait until time for the luncheon. I concentrated with diligence, getting my act together so I could take it on the road. I dressed in a navy blue dress (the same color blue used in the word *Mobil*, written across the front of my hardhat). I wore a pair of very nice heels, grabbed my briefcase, and tore out to the meeting. Just before I walked into the luncheon I placed the hardhat firmly on my head, gave it a slight tilt to the right, and put a piece of chewing gum in my mouth to add to my air of nonchalant assurance. Then I walked in.

Just inside the door, a number of models in a style show had gathered, awaiting their turn to walk across a room of nicely-arranged tables at which groups of fashionable women with well-coifed hair were seated, enjoying lunch . . . about two hundred women in all. At first no one paid any attention to me or my imposing appearance. After all, I had just arrived and was obscured by this network of backstage activity. For all they knew, perhaps I was going to model the latest fashion to wear with hardhats!

Momentarily, Marilyn, who was seated at the head table, saw me. The look on her face was priceless. Words cannot do it justice, but let me try. Have you ever seen someone who looked as though they had been goosed by an electric prod? Well, that's the way she looked. Shocked. Stunned. Confused. Often I had heard Marilyn use the phrase, "They looked as though they had been goosed by an electric prod," and I always thought it was so funny because it produced such a vivid mental picture. Now she was living out one of her favorite verbal descriptions . . . she was the one who had been goosed.

Although I was screaming within to laugh, if for no other reason than for the look on her face, I didn't dare. In fact, I stoically managed to appear utterly indifferent to the entire congregation of women who were enjoying their scheduled activities, and went right on chewing my gum. The style show ladies, exhibiting a degree of irritation, walked around me to continue lining up for their part of the program. But I never moved—just stood steadfast, right in the middle of the entrance, with cocked hat, pretty dress, dark glasses, and briefcase.

Finally a lady from the head table, after her curiosity had undoubtedly gotten the best of her, approached me and asked if there was anything she could do for me. Was there some way she could help me? "Oh, no thank you," I answered with an impeded nasal twang. "I'm fine." Looking a little confused, the lady returned to the head table, which by now could be characterized by that biblical phrase of "murmurings and disputings." I began to read their lips—"Who is she?" "What does she want?" "Is she some kind of an official?"

During all this Marilyn could have won an Academy Award for her facial expressions alone. Every second they were different, constantly changing from strained control to near collapse. She was marvelous, and before I knew it I was actually having the time of my life. I decided that since I had come this far, I might as well go the whole nine yards. When the style show was over, before the special music began, I walked into the room and went to the back so I could lean against the wall in order to get a better view of the head table, as well as to appear more official—more knowledgeable of my reason for being there.

Those poor women; bless their innocent hearts. They didn't know what to do. Intermittently they would look at me strangely, then look away hurriedly because no one knew for sure who I was and why I was there. I would say it was collectively the most baffled look I have ever seen on a group of women in my life. When the singer performed, I took off my hardhat and covered my heart. When the announcements were given, I took deliberate and obvious notes. In short, I entered in fully, just as my challenge required, and never once blew my cover. But the funniest part was yet to come.

After general consternation and several attempts from various women to help me or learn my true identity and purpose in being there, I caught Marilyn's eye to mouth that my thirty minutes were up and I was going home. I could hear inaudible strains of a victory march being played in my heart and I felt triumphant. "Oh, Hobbitt . . . here we come!" But just as I got Marilyn's attention, she was being introduced as the speaker. She quickly motioned me to wait a few moments, that she wanted to say something about me to the group. So I leaned back against the wall and obeyed. By now I had won anyway.

She stood behind the podium. "Ladies, before I begin," she said, "I have been tremendously curious about the roving lady in the Mobil hardhat. Have you?" Everyone, en masse, turned then and looked straight at me. I nodded with a slight smile. She went on, gesturing toward me, "Is there anything we can do for you or is there a question that perhaps we could answer?"

With all the dignity and aplomb I could muster, I stepped forward about four or five feet, and in a loud, pronouncedly defective voice I announced to the mesmerized audience that I was with Mobil Oil Corporation and we were going to be digging a trench in front of the building momentarily. Some of their cars were in the way and would have to be moved. I told them the digging crew would not begin until I gave them the word, and since the speaker looked rather longwinded to me, I had decided to wait until she finished before I called out a list of license numbers of cars which would be affected. Then I proceeded to list off some fictitious license numbers which I had already written on the back of a card.

Marilyn, by now, could stand it no longer and absolutely fell apart. She literally lost her breath laughing. While many of the other women joined her (those who all the while had probably been secretly giggling within themselves anyway), others felt either worried that they couldn't remember their license number, or sorry for my unfortunate speech impediment and didn't want to make fun of me. After a bit, Marilyn gathered herself together and introduced me, for real, and explained to the group our ludicrous bet of a few days earlier and how she never in a million years expected me to take her up on the challenge. "But I have found out Luci will do anything for a free meal," she said, still laughing. There was a slight pause, then everyone broke into enthusiastic applause as I gave the "Rocky" victory sign. In my normal voice, I thanked them all for being so very gracious about the whole thing and assured them that all their cars were safe. Smiling to the group, I turned around and walked out. As the door closed behind me, the sound of their continued applause and laughter rang in my ears. Such a nice sound.

Eight months later, the evening at The Hobbitt became a reality. It was all we had anticipated—just great! Marilyn once again acknowledged her utter surprise at my bravery and ability to allow my dignity to be reduced by such daring and fearless behavior. "Well, Marilyn," I said, "what are friends for, anyway?"

For the most part, the very best times I have had in life have been with my friends. But I hasten to add, the most difficult and painful experiences I have endured have also been because of my friends. Being friends and having friends places upon the human heart some of its greatest and most profound requirements. And I believe one of the reasons we are given friends in this life, or the reason we are permitted to be friends with someone else, is that that state of being exacts from us such pronounced and defined emotions. Friends unconsciously teach us a lot about living, simply because of what we feel for them and what they feel for us. To put it briefly, that's what friends are for.

Recently I was glancing through an old book I have, entitled *The Beauties of Friendship*. Originally it had been given to one of my father's cousins around the turn of the century, and shortly before her death some seventy years later she gave it to me. The book is an interesting collection of poetry, quotations, and comments on the subject of friendship. Some of them are beautiful and truly worth remembering, such as this excerpt from a sermon given by the highly respected Roman Catholic Cardinal, James Gibbons:

> Among the blessings and enjoyments of this life, there are few that can be compared in value to the possession of a faithful friend, who will pour the truth into your heart though you may wince under it—of a friend who will defend you when you are unjustly assailed by the tongues of calumny, who will not forsake you when you have fallen into disgrace, who will counsel you in your doubts and perplexities, who will open his purse and aid you without expecting any return of his favors, who will rejoice at your prosperity and grieve at your adversity, who will bear half of your burden—who will add to your joys, and diminish your sorrows by sharing in both.
>
> The Holy Scripture, in the following passage, describes the value of a loyal friend: "A faithful friend is a strong defense, and he who has found him hath found a treasure. Nothing can be compared to a faithful

friend, and no weight of gold or silver is able to countervail the goodness of his fidelity. A faithful friend is the medicine of life and immortality, and they that fear God shall find him."[1]

There is no doubt about it, faithful friends are treasures indeed, and I thank God for those he has given to me. They stand out like beacons of light scattered across a hillside of long shadows, and the warmth of their light aids me in finding direction, feeling more secure about what lies ahead, or knowing that if I need to retreat, they will be there to welcome me home, even if I feel defeated. Is there any substitute for that sense of fidelity?

Take Marilyn, for instance. Dozens of times she has picked up my battered psyche and with her humor, her love, her loyalty, and her honesty, she has patched it back into shape. When I have had false or idealistic dreams about what lay ahead, she has, with her penchant for reality and clarity, helped me to come back down to earth in order to deal with what is—what is real, what is feasible, what is best. Although it's been terribly painful at times, she's done it without deflating my self-respect or destroying my courage to move ahead. This trait of truthfulness is a quality of value in friendship I admire greatly, and one which Solomon lauds in Proverbs 27:6: "Wounds from a friend are better than kisses from an enemy."

Or take Julius. Julius Karoblis offers his friends one of life's sweetest morsels—tenacity. His friendship will simply not let me go. Having come to this country in 1963 from Uruguay, South America, Julius spoke very little English, but that seemed to be no deterrent to his will to accomplish something with his life and his desire to make friends. He and I have had many philosophical discussions, and we have talked for hours about our individual dreams and hopes. He has said to me, "My favorite thing about America is that she is not afraid to fight, to get involved." When Julius considers the words in our national anthem, ". . . the land of the free, and the home of the brave," he

---

1. Samuel Francis Woolard, ed., *The Beauties of Friendship* (Wichita: The Goldsmith-Woolard Publishing Company, 1909), p. 16.

takes that as truth. He is the bravest man I have ever known, I believe, yet he has that tender side which makes it hard for him to say no when someone he loves will be affected.

His tenacity, however, is not only characteristic in friendships. Julius has diligently pursued a degree in graphic arts since he has been in America and now lacks only nineteen hours of having his master's. At the age of forty-five he bought a car and learned to drive. He has worked for the same company for fifteen years and has participated as a supernumerary with the San Francisco Opera for the past fourteen years. He says that his motto for life, if he had one, would be "Don't Be Afraid," and that his happiest moments are when he is with people he loves.

I have observed Julius, on more than one occasion, to have valid reason for giving up on a friendship. I have known of times when his kindness and generosity of spirit were taken advantage of. Nevertheless, he has held firm—has loved regardless of the hardship, has refused to abandon his friends for any reason. I am even aware of occasions when false accusations were made against him and he remained friendly toward his accusers. Once, in conversation, Julius confessed that he thought the worst thing one human being could do to another was to betray a trust. Tenacity in Julius is one of his many endearing qualities.

Doesn't Solomon also encourage that in friendship in Proverbs 27, verse 10? "Never abandon a friend—either yours or your father's. Then you won't need to go to a distant relative for help in your time of need."

Or let's take Cyndi as an example. Remember when Cardinal Gibbons said, "A friend [is one] . . . who will rejoice at your prosperity and grieve at your adversity"? It can easily be said that this quality is epitomized in Cyndi Monroe. Rarely have I known anyone who could without jealousy enter into my prosperity, or without smugness enter into my adversity. Somehow she has the happy and enviable faculty to meet me where I am, entering in completely with true and sincere empathy. This tasteful ability of Cyndi's to distinguish the flavor of my mood and to perceive what is appropriate to say or do makes her invaluable as my friend. It seems she has a sixth sense about how to address an issue at hand. In that she is a lively, playful, witty, supportive conversationalist, or a quiet, attentive, sensitive listener. Solomon even praises that quality in friendship in verse 17 of the same chapter: "A friendly discussion is as stimulating as the sparks that fly when iron strikes iron."

For the fourth item on my list of qualities that makes a friend a treasure, let me refer you to Sandy Lough. A few years ago, Sandy and I were having lunch and I could tell her heart was burdened about something. She was warm and friendly, of course, which is in keeping with her usual manner, but I sensed she was a bit withdrawn. Without wanting to pry, I carefully inquired what might be troubling her. Little by little, in complete honesty and trust, she revealed her heart to me. It was a precious time for us both because it opened a door to an even deeper friendship. In fact, because of her transparency, I felt free and invited to be very candid with Sandy about a problem in my own life that I had held within for fear of being misunderstood or rejected. Her openness evoked the same from me. Since then, our mutual friendship has proven to be high on the scale of priorities when it comes to people we can trust and enjoy being with. Later that year, for my birthday, she composed this poem and presented it to me:

> I called you a national treasure
> one time when you opened your heart;
> You let me in and you comforted me
> when my world had fallen apart.
>
> To know you were out there and caring
> meant far more than you'll ever know.
>
> You made me feel that I mattered,
> that though shattered, I would mend and grow.
>
> You are gold—one of God's finer creatures
> and although I've told you before,
> it bears saying again,
> I love you, dear friend.
>
> Each year more and more . . .
> more and more.

Solomon referred to a transparent reflection in friendship, in verse 19 of Proverbs 27: "A mirror reflects a man's face, but what he is really like is shown by the kind of friends he chooses."

What are friends for, anyway? I believe they are in our lives to point out the value of important qualities we look for in other people as well as want in ourselves. First, truthfulness—that honest, sincere, genuine confirmation of the facts as being real and what I must deal with. Second, tenacity—the strength of character to hold firm to what I know is bedrock in a relationship when the structure is being threatened by winds of betrayal, false accusations, or personal advantage. Third, tastefulness—the ability to notice, appreciate, evaluate, and enter into what is beautiful, appropriate, or needful . . . and to do it without jealousy or smugness. And fourth, transparency—the quality of openness; letting the cracks show in our lives and welcoming disclosure of heartaches or burdens from other people. If we can ever master these attributes, we will have all the friends we can possibly want, and we will be to others as Gibbons noted: "the medicine of life and immortality."

Kazantzakis said at the beginning of this chapter, "A goodly number of pleasures have fallen my lot in the course of a lifetime; I have no reason to complain." Neither do I. Within that "goodly number of pleasures" I would have to silently name many wonderful, faithful friends, of whose number you have just read about four. They have loved me deeply; they have given me immeasurable joys; they have taught me much. Sometimes the going has been rough and we've butted our heads together to work through tough issues. But we've made it, and the rewards have been worth the battles.

Besides, I don't mind locking horns occasionally with somebody I love. Remember, I'm the one with the hardhat.

MY MENTORS

To obey a harsh signal and abandon ourselves with confidence to the high forces around and within us, visible and invisible, unshakable in our faith that these know everything and we nothing—this is the one and only road to fertility. All the others are sterile and deceptive, because they do not lead anywhere, but simply bring us back to the miserable, accursed self after vain and presumptuous meanderings.

Although I am embarrassed to do so, I would like to make a personal confession: I did not learn to read until I was thirty. Does that shock you? Well, let me explain. I knew the alphabet, of course, and I was acquainted with many words, but I didn't know how to read with an eye of discernment. By the time I was thirty (twenty years ago), I had been a college graduate for eight years and had done my share of required reading for school. I had also availed myself of certain books which lay within my extra-curricular fields of interest: art, music, travel, crafts, history. But to have been considered "a reader" in the acceptable sense of the phrase would have been erroneous. To me, one who has earned that auspicious title is one who has learned to read with associative thinking. He or she has the mental acumen to perceive not only the words of the writer but the underlying message to the reader. This type of reading consists of more than understanding facts to enhance knowledge; it is reading with an eye for insights, to enhance character. It is the ability to see and understand the inner nature of things, and where applicable to identify and apply these in one's own experience. That's what I mean by reading with associative thinking, and that's what I did not do until I was thirty.

Now before I horrify you, unwittingly perhaps, with other embarrassing confessions, let me clarify one major point. When I turned thirty, I had been a Christian for seventeen years, having accepted the Lord as my personal Savior at the age of thirteen. I had read and studied the Bible for all those years, off and on to varying degrees of intensity, only to be matched with the same degree of growth in my Christian experience. In other words, I was able to read and understand certain scriptures with some discernment (albeit questionable at times, as evidenced by my behavior), but I never felt I could "take credit," as it were, for this ability to discern. In my way of thinking, and from what I had been taught, the credit belonged to God's Spirit, the One who teaches the child of God and illumines areas of darkness in his or her life. Not only had I been taught this by my earthly Bible teachers, but the Word of God itself made that clear in passages such as these words of Jesus in John 14:26:

> But when the Father sends the Comforter instead of me—and by the Comforter I mean the Holy Spirit—he will teach you much, as well as remind you of everything I myself have told you.

In fact, it is the Holy Spirit himself who confirms that we belong to God: "For his Holy Spirit speaks to us deep in our hearts, and tells us that we really are God's children."

I'm telling you this to point out the fact that while I was spending years reading without discernment in my liberal education—that type of learning which comes to the mind through exposure to knowledge and skill—I was at the same time reading the Bible with discernment (thanks to the teaching ministry of the Holy Spirit), and I was enjoying a spiritual education which was quite apart from my own efforts. While I am ashamed to confess that my liberal arts education did not begin in depth until twenty years ago, I don't want you to think that for all of my life I was totally devoid of good judgment or perceptions about the importance of one's growth of character. The Holy Spirit took care of that, so I think it is correct to say he was my first Mentor. Interestingly enough, the ardent English Baptist minister and celebrated preacher, Charles Haddon Spurgeon, said in one of his sermons, "The Bible should be our mentor," and indeed it should.

Before we go further, let me define *mentor* as I am using it, so that this definition will serve as the foundation stone upon which I build my following thoughts. Originally the Greek word *mentor* was used in Homer's epic poem, *The Odyssey*, which recounts the adventure of its hero, Odysseus (or Ulysses to us), as he makes his way home to Ithaca after the Trojan war. Ulysses had a son with the long Greek name of Telemachus, whom he left in the care of his old, trusted friend, Mentor, when Ulysses went off to war about ten years before the narrative begins. Mentor appears prominently at the beginning of *The Odyssey*, and his name has become synonymous with a wise and faithful counselor. Commonly, *mentor* is a noun, defined as an experienced and trusted adviser or counselor.

Since it is my purpose in this chapter to acquaint you with my mentors, I want to introduce them to you individually as the four people who have counseled me wisely for the past twenty years from the pages of their writings. Although we have never met face to face, I feel that I know them through their books and philosophies. They have not only opened my eyes to the incomparable value of reading with perceptive comprehension, but by the application of their counsel upon my experience, their words of wisdom have been used by God as his instruments to forge out some of the positive alterations that have taken place in my heart and in my attitude toward life as a whole. I have not always agreed with their theology or lack of it, nor have I fully supported every cause they have embraced. Nevertheless, the radical arguments of their beliefs have made me think deeply about my own, often challenging me to creative action.

In the case of my Mentors, their ambivalent approach to living, as expressed in their writing, has enabled them to offer their readers an almost kaleidoscopic view of experiences. For instance, in their own involvements they have known duality: joys and sorrows, peace and turmoil, liberty and bondage, light and darkness. And they have come to understand that the rich life must have both—it is characterized by what is absolute as well as relative. Consequently, these writers were able to differentiate between essence and appearance . . . that very delicate balance which separates and identifies two important poles in living and decision making: what is eternal and what is temporal.

Every one of these men writes from this point of view, and while individually they may hold personal opinions and preferences, none of them passes judgment or goes immediately to a solution. It is as though, by living out these principles I have just mentioned, they've come to realize that very little in life is black or white, and much in life falls within the area of gray. Their insights have helped me form my principles for living, and if this were the only value in their writing, that would be enough to qualify them as my Mentors. But there's so much more.

By way of introduction, then, let me acquaint you with the members of this distinguished cast. Collectively, their lives cover a span of 108 years, and for 54 of those years they were all living at the same time—in different places on the earth. The last of the four died in May, 1983. All of them were men, each born in a different European country: Alsace (now part of France), Germany, England, and Greece. Highly educated, two were Nobel Prize winners, and a third was a nominee. They traveled widely, were fluent in more than one language, and together they represented the fields of art, music, theology, education, law, government, philosophy, medicine, and literature.

Following is a brief outline of their individual credentials.

Albert Schweitzer (1875-1965). An Alsatian philosopher, musician, theologian, and medical missionary in Lambarene, Gabon (French Equatorial Africa), Albert Schweitzer received a doctorate in philosophy at the age of twenty-four, a doctorate in theology at twenty-five, and a doctorate in medicine at thirty-eight. He was an accomplished organist and a recognized authority on the works of Bach. At the age of thirty-seven he married a scholar who was also a trained nurse, and together they built their own hospital in Africa, where for the most part he devoted his life. Schweitzer authored many books, several of which expounded his belief in the full development of human resources, and he believed this principle to be essential to the survival of civilization. For his efforts in behalf of "The Brotherhood of Nations," he was awarded the Nobel Peace Prize. He died at the age of ninety.

Hermann Hesse (1877-1962). German-born Hesse was a novelist, an essayist, and a poet, all rolled into one. He had a burgeoning imagination and a lively, engaging, lucid writing style with a tendency to combine the ideas of widely-varying times and cultures into a single whole. His novels are characterized by a distinctive and personal view of humanity with its common dilemmas: themes such as "absolute freedom involves a sense of guilt," "any true freedom must be an inner one," "if meditation has value it must give way to commitment," "learn what must be taken seriously and laugh at the rest," and "war is the outward manifestation of a great inner revolution in a world whose values have collapsed." In 1946 Hesse won the Nobel Prize for Literature with the final novel of his life, *The Glass Bead Game*, whose underlying theme is the affectionate, tolerant acceptance of human reality and its limitations. During Hesse's lifetime of eighty-five years, he received hundreds of letters from students and admirers all over the world who took his novels as an invitation to pour out their hearts to him. Had I realized who he was earlier in my life, I'm sure I would have done the same, but I didn't become aware of his work until the year he died.

Kenneth Clark (1903-1983). At the age of seven, British-born Kenneth Clark discovered his ability to recognize and enjoy works of art, and from then on it was the moving force in his life. In fact, he held so many important positions in the art and cultural life of his country, he was called its Minister of Culture. After his education at Winchester and Trinity College, Oxford, he became director of the National Gallery in London and Surveyor of the King's Pictures. Recipient of many honorary degrees, he was also chairman of the Arts Council of Great Britain and professor of Fine Art at Oxford. He is the author of numerous books and essays on art, the best known of which was made into a series of thirteen fifty-two-minute color films, initially for television: *Civilisation: A Personal View*. You'd think that anyone who could write a book and title it that would automatically command some kind of authority and respect, wouldn't you?

Before I go on to my fourth Mentor, let me tell you an amusing story which accompanies my reading of one of Clark's analytical books on art, entitled *The Nude*, a beautifully-written 475-page volume considering how the nude, as a study in ideal form, dominated sculpture and painting for many years. It is a marvelous book, incidentally, full of photographs of nudes, and written in Clark's witty and intelligent style. My copy is a thick paperback that I bought in 1970, and it is marked with my own ballpoint notes and scribbles. During the many weeks it took to complete the reading of the book, I was summoned to jury duty. You know how that can be—hours in the central jury room waiting to be called (maybe) to various courtrooms for empaneling by the lawyers. Since it was my custom never to go anywhere without a book in hand when I knew waiting would be involved, I carried along *The Nude* daily. Very early each morning during those hours in the central jury room, I became immersed in its pages, often making copious notes in the margins. One morning near the end of the week, an elderly woman with a sweet countenance, whom I had noticed watching me from time to time throughout my days there, sat by me as I was reading. She leaned over to me and whispered, "I beg your pardon, but are you on a porno case?"

"I'm sorry; what did you ask?"

"Are you on a pornographic court case?" she repeated. "I keep seeing you with this book called *The Nude* and I thought that maybe you got that in one of the courtrooms as information about the case or something."

Well, I couldn't resist. "Yes, I am," I replied, "and it's a mess, too. Lots of naked bodies that the lawyer wanted us to have the facts about. But I really can't talk with you about it. You know how these attorneys are. They tell you to keep your mouth shut."

"Gosh," she said, "what an interesting case that must be. All I ever get is drunk driving."

"Me too, usually, but this time it's really a dilly . . . 'scuse me, I gotta run," and I left in order to keep from laughing.

I thought later how much Kenneth Clark would have enjoyed that story. I should have written him about it and shared my amusement, because he certainly supplied me with many laughs through the years. In May, 1983, Lord Clark died at the age of seventy-nine. It was truly a loss to the world of art analysis and to our civilization. As my dear art-loving friend Kurt Ratican once said, "Kenneth Clark is one of the few art historians who sees art in its proper perspective as being a reflection of history, filling the function of a camera, but also with its own emotions, humor, and intelligences."

Nikos Kazantzakis (1883-1957). Of course, by now you are familiar with this particular Mentor because the title of the book you are holding, as you know, is based upon a quotation taken from a volume of his, entitled *Report to Greco*. But just a few notes about his life. Kazantzakis was a Greek poet and novelist, born on the island of Crete. He received a doctorate of law from the University of Athens and was widely traveled. He mastered five modern languages as well as Latin and ancient and modern Greek. His writings (the best known of which is *Zorba the Greek*), heavily influenced by personal conflicts between the flesh and the spirit and the philosophies of Dante, Bergson, Lenin, Buddha, and Nietzsche, have been translated into some thirty languages. Probably his greatest literary outcry was the passionate, often tragic search for freedom. Kazantzakis died at age seventy-four, exhausted of all adventures and all theories. On his tombstone in Herakleion, Crete, the following words have been engraved: "I do not hope for anything. I do not fear anything. I am free."

There they are: my four Mentors in a nutshell. Volumes have been written by and about each of these individuals, so to attempt to reduce their attributes and achievements to these few paragraphs is almost ludicrous. Should you desire more information, biographies and their own works are plentiful.

When one reads much of the fiction, non-fiction, poetry, or essays of any of the above-mentioned authors, one soon perceives, intertwined and inescapable, numerous concepts, truths, and principles threaded throughout their works. They are trying to say something important to humanity and they want their readers to perceive their messages. They have said so much to me, causing me to think about my life—its direction, its brevity, its scope, its quality—and they have also caused me to think about my death, which will come soon enough. But before I tell you what I think they have said to me as I have read their words, let me give you some brief examples of their writings.

Admittedly, these examples are taken out of context, but that should not matter as you read, because I have chosen excerpts which are not dependent upon the paragraphs or story line surrounding them. These examples are minuscule snapshots of the enormous picture of their messages.

We'll start with Albert Schweitzer.

The question which haunts men and women today is whether life is worth living. Perhaps each of us has had the experience of talking with a friend one day, finding that person bright, happy, apparently in the full joy of life; and then the next day we find that he has taken his own life! Stoicism has brought us to this point, by driving out the fear of death; for, by inference it suggests that we are free to choose whether to live or not. But if we entertain such a possibility, we do so by ignoring the melody of the will-to-live, which compels us to face the mystery, the value, the high trust committed to us in life. We may not understand it, but we begin to appreciate its great value. Therefore, when we find those who relinquish life, while we may not condemn them, we do pity them for having ceased to be in possession of themselves. Ultimately, the issue is not whether we do or do not fear death. The real issue is that of reverence for life.[1]

---

1. Albert Schweitzer, *Albert Schweitzer: An Anthology* (Boston: The Beacon Press, 1947), pp. 255-256.

Another example from Schweitzer shows his reverence for life, the reverence for any living being that he refers to as the "real issue" in the example above.

> A deep impression was made on me by something which happened during my seventh or eighth year. Henry Brasch and I had with strips of india rubber made ourselves catapults, with which we could shoot small stones. It was spring and the end of Lent, when one morning Henry said to me, "Come along, let's go on to the Redberg and shoot some birds." This was to me a terrible proposal, but I did not venture to refuse for fear he should laugh at me. We got close to a tree which was still without any leaves, and on which the birds were singing beautifully to greet the morning, without showing the least fear of us. Then stooping like a red Indian hunter, my companion put a bullet in the leather of his catapult and took aim. In obedience to his nod of command, I did the same, though with terrible twinges of conscience, vowing to myself that I would shoot directly he did. At that very moment the church bells began to ring, mingling their music with the songs of the birds and the sunshine. It was the warning bell, which began half an hour before the regular peal ringing, and for me it was a voice from heaven. I shooed the birds away, so that they flew where they were safe from my companion's catapult, and then I fled home. And ever since then, when the Passiontide bells ring out to the leafless trees and the sunshine, I reflect with a rush of grateful emotion how on that day their music drove deep into my heart the commandment: "Thou shall not kill."[2]

The following words of Hermann Hesse address a philosophical concept I have toyed with for many years, namely that no matter how permanent we may feel, we are always in a state of transition, and as long as we live, we'll be in some phase of that state.

---

2. *Albert Schweitzer*, pp. 274-275.

God is perfect being. Everything else that exists is only half, only a part, is becoming, is mixed, is made up of potentialities. But God is not mixed. He is one, he has no potentialities, but is the total, the complete reality. Whereas we are transitory, we are becoming, we are potentials; there is no perfection to deed, from possibility to realization, we participate in true being, become by a degree more similar to the perfect and divine. That is what it means to realize oneself.[3]

Or here he talks about patience:

Patience is the most difficult thing of all and the only thing that is worth learning. All nature, all growth, all peace, everything that flowers and is beautiful in the world depends on patience, requires time, silence, trust, and faith in the long-term processes which far exceed any single lifetime, which are accessible to the insight of no one person, and which in their totality can be experienced only by peoples and epochs, not by individuals.[4]

An example of Hesse's poetry, written at the end of 1914, conveys the struggle and brevity of life as well as the surety of death that is housed in every soul. He calls it "To Children":

You know nothing of time,
You know only that, somewhere in the distance,
A war is being fought,
You whittle your wood into sword and shield and
    spear
And play your game blissfully in the garden,
Set up your tents,
Carry white bandages marked with the red cross.
And if my wish for you has any power,
So war will remain
For you, always, only a dim legend,

---

3. Hermann Hesse, *Narcissus and Goldmund* (New York: Farrar, Straus and Giroux, Inc., 1968), p. 280.

4. Hermann Hesse, *Reflections* (New York: Farrar, Straus and Giroux, Inc., 1974), p. 58.

So you will never stand in the field
And never die
And never rush out of a house crumbling in fire.

Nevertheless, you will be soldiers one day
And one day you will know
That the sweet breath of this life,
The precious possession of the heartbeat,
Is only a loan, and that whatever was lost
In the past, and the heir you long for,
And the farthest future,
Rolls through your blood,
And that for every hair on your head
Somebody endured one struggle, one pain, one death.

And you shall know that whatever is noble
In your soul is always a warrior,
Even though he bears no weapons,
That every day a struggle and a destiny is waiting.
Do not forget this!
Think of the blood, the shambles, the ruin
On which your future reposes,
And how, even more, upon death and sacrifice is
    builded
The tiniest happiness.

Then your life will flame out more
And one day gather even death
Into its arms.[5]

Kenneth Clark's all-encompassing achievement, *Civilisation*, comprised a history of all the things that have served to shape Western Man: his arts, his architecture, his philosophy, his technical achievement. The book and the television series were works of genius, through the magic and charm of Clark's unique imagination. He built bridges over time and space and he did it with analysis, wit, and incisiveness. Nevertheless, at

---

5. From *Poems* by Hermann Hesse, selected and translated by James Wright. Copyright © 1970 by James Wright. Reprinted by permission of Farrar, Straus and Giroux, Inc.

the close of his magnum opus, after covering centuries of humanity's finest accomplishments with his sensitive eye and verbal skill, Lord Clark left us with his simple but profound creed:

> At this point I reveal myself in my true colors, as a stick-in-the-mud. I hold a number of beliefs that have been repudiated by the liveliest intellects of our time. I believe that order is better than chaos, creation better than destruction. I prefer gentleness to violence, forgiveness to vendetta. On the whole I think that knowledge is preferable to ignorance, and I am sure that human sympathy is more valuable than ideology. I believe that in spite of the recent triumphs of science, men haven't changed much in the last two thousand years; and in consequence we must still try to learn from history. History is ourselves. I also hold one or two beliefs that are more difficult to put shortly. For example, I believe in courtesy, the ritual by which we avoid hurting other people's feelings by satisfying our own egos. And I think we should remember that we are part of a great whole, which for convenience we call nature. All living things are our brothers and sisters. Above all, I believe in the God-given genius of certain individuals, and I value a society that makes their existence possible.[6]

You have been reading quotations from Nikos Kazantzakis throughout this book. They begin every chapter and divide the two parts, so you are somewhat familiar with his words and his message. Therefore, in closing these examples, let me leave you with only two final excerpts from his thoughts. First, this:

> Once, I remembered, I had detached a chrysalis from the trunk of an olive tree and placed it in my palm. Inside the transparent coating I discerned a living thing. It was moving. The hidden process must have reached its terminus; the future, still-enslaved butter-

---

6. Kenneth Clark, *Civilisation, A Personal View* (New York: Harper & Row, 1969), pp. 346-347.

fly was waiting with silent tremors for the sacred hour when it would emerge into the sunlight. It was not in a hurry. Having confidence in the light, the warm air, in God's eternal law, it was waiting.

But I was in a hurry. I wanted to see the miracle hatch before me as soon as possible, wanted to see how the body surges out of its tomb and shroud to become a soul. Bending over, I began to blow my warm breath over the chrysalis, and behold! a slit soon incised itself on the chrysalis's back, the entire shroud gradually split from top to bottom, and the immature, bright green butterfly appeared, still tightly locked together, its wings twisted, its legs glued to its abdomen. It squirmed gently and kept coming more and more to life beneath my warm, persistent breath. One wing as pale as a budding poplar leaf disengaged itself from the body and began to palpitate, struggling to unfold along its entire length, but in vain. It stayed half opened, shriveled. Soon the other wing moved as well, toiled in its own right to stretch, was unable to, and remained half unfolded and trembling. I, with a human being's effrontery, continued to lean over and blow my warm exhalation upon the maimed wings, but they had ceased to move now and had drooped down, as stiff and lifeless as stone.

I felt sick at heart. Because of my hurry, because I had dared to transgress an eternal law, I had killed the butterfly. In my hand I held a carcass. Years and years have passed, but that butterfly's carcass has weighed heavily on my conscience ever since.

Man hurries, God does not. That is why man's works are uncertain and maimed, while God's are flawless and sure. My eyes welling with tears, I vowed never to transgress this eternal law again. Like a tree I would be blasted by wind, struck by sun and rain, and would wait with confidence; the long-desired hour of flowering and fruit would come.[7]

7. Nikos Kazantzakis, *Report to Greco* (New York: Simon and Schuster, 1961) p. 449.

Then, this:

> Let us unite, let us hold each other tightly, let us
> merge our hearts, let us create—so long as the warmth
> of this earth endures, so long as no earthquakes,
> cataclysms, icebergs or comets come to destroy us—
> let us create for Earth a brain and a heart, let us give a
> human meaning to the superhuman struggle.[8]

Let's say now, in an effort to reach a sense of clarity and closure, that I provide us with a hypothetical situation. It's a Sunday afternoon at 3:00 and I am sitting in my living room with all
four of my Mentors. They have lived the greater part of their
lives—they're in their seventies by now and I am at my present
age of fifty. I have just said to them, "Gentlemen, I've been reading your books for twenty years and I have not only enjoyed them
and benefited from them, but they have, to a greater or lesser degree, changed my life. Will you please tell me in plain English the
essence of your beliefs and your writings, in the most succinct
way possible, because I want to share with others what I have
learned from you." Here is what I believe would be their answer
collectively:

> Luci, life has been given to you as a gift. It is a pre-
> cious, mysterious world that has been entrusted to
> you by God, and your greatest challenge is to enjoy,
> develop, appreciate, protect, and treasure that gift
> with everything you've got. Abandon yourself to it and
> don't hold back. Life comes in stages and it is your
> responsibility and your joy to love life in every stage.
> Living fully and completely means struggle and ten-
> sion. It means dealing with opposing inner and outer
> forces, but even that is part of the beautiful mystery,
> Luci, because your love of life will be in exact propor-
> tion to what it has required from you and what you
> have willingly given. It will teach you kindness, love,
> patience, wisdom, goodness, tolerance—when you

8. Nikos Kazantzakis, *The Saviors of God, Spiritual Exercises* (New York: Simon and Schuster, 1960), p. 55.

learn to stop fighting against the struggle—and your life will then have real value.

One day death will come. It is coming to each one of us and we must all say yes to it. But death is not bad. It is not an enemy. Death is a friend, calling us out of the heart of love—it is simply another form of life, the final stage . . . and Luci, it will usher you into real freedom.

That is sound advice from my Mentors. Their message and their encouragement have helped me immeasurably. The application of their principles to my experience has made life worth living, and they have only confirmed the message and the encouragement received from my first Mentors, God's Holy Spirit and his written Word, which says:

He has given you the whole world to use, and life and even death are your servants. He has given you all of the present and all of the future. All are yours, and you belong to Christ, and Christ is God's.[9]

I have always been fascinated by epitaphs. When I was much younger, I enjoyed reading them at random throughout cemeteries. Some inscriptions were very short, others quite long. But in either case, they usually attempted to give a verbal portrayal of the essence of the individual whose bones lay in that spot. I have often pondered my own epitaph—what did I want it to say? What was the truth about my character? How did I want to live my life and face my death so that my epitaph would be a reflection of my philosophy?

Then one day, some twenty years ago now, I read Irving Stone's lengthy fictional novel, *The Agony and the Ecstasy,* which is based upon the historical facts surrounding the life of Michelangelo. I loved the book! And it was the volume that caused me, for the very first time, to read associatively. Near the end of it I found a great quotation, one that I thought would make a superb inscription on my tombstone because it so captures my philosophy of life:

---

9. 1 Corinthians 3:22-23.

Life has been good. God did not create me to abandon me. I have loved marble, yes, and paint, too. I have loved architecture, and poetry . . . I have loved my family and friends. I have loved God, the forms of the earth and the heavens, and people. I have loved life to the full, and now I love death as its natural termination.[10]

---

10. Irving Stone, *The Agony and the Ecstasy* (New York: Doubleday & Company, Inc., 1961), p. 754.

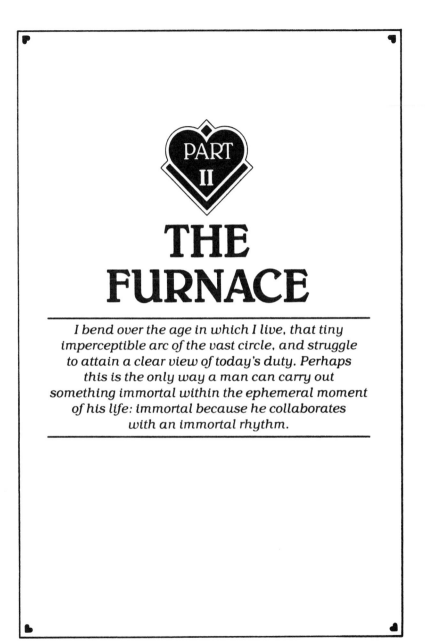

PART II

THE FURNACE

I bend over the age in which I live, that tiny imperceptible arc of the vast circle, and struggle to attain a clear view of today's duty. Perhaps this is the only way a man can carry out something immortal within the ephemeral moment of his life: immortal because he collaborates with an immortal rhythm.

SCHOOL

*I did not know what I was going to do with my life;
before anything else I wanted to find an answer,
my answer, to the timeless questions, and then after
that I would decide what I would become. If I did
not begin by discovering what was the grand
purpose of life on earth, I said to myself, how would
I be able to discover the purpose of my tiny
ephemeral life? And if I did not give my life a
purpose, how would I be able to engage in action?*

How many of you remember that accursed time in your life when you first encountered "word problems"? For me, and I assume for most Americans, that would have been the sixth grade. A word problem went something like this:

> Fred got on the school bus in front of his house with three apples. After the bus went four blocks, Mary got on with two apples and sat by Fred. In casual conversation, they rode six blocks, where they stopped to pick up Amy and Pam, who got on each eating an apple. After continuing four and one-half city blocks, the bus came to a stop and let off all its passengers at school. How many miles was it from Fred's house to school?

Now, all the while I am reading the problem, I'm diligently counting apples and blocks and waiting for one of the characters to say something of value which will give me a clue to the upcoming question, but to no avail. The question might as well have been, "What day was it?" The whole thing seemed to make no sense to me and I resented the fact that the author tricked me into believing the problem was going to be related to words, not numbers, because after all it was called a "word problem." "Who needs this anyway?" I would say to myself. "I'm never going to use information like this when I'm grown. Adults don't care how far Fred lives from the school, and besides, when I'm the age of my parents, Fred will probably have moved, and the question will have a wrong answer . . ." Typical of me, always trying to work through the logistics of the issue, rather than to see its value from a mathematical point of view.

Realizing that word problems were going to be the beginning of my scholastic ruination, I went to my father in my need and reported that unless something was done very quickly to enlarge my brain power, I was never going to graduate to junior high school. That would have been a fate worse than death because I was following in the footsteps of an older brother whose academic record was not only one of all A's, but whose highest achievements were in the field of math. My father was also good in math, but his time did not permit the concentrated attention to it that I required, so he assigned Orville, my older brother, the duty of being my mathematical pedagogue. That *was* a fate worse than death! Orville's computer-like mind, coupled with his youth (he was only thirteen months older than I, you will recall), as well as his multi-faceted interests in his own pursuits, left him little time or concern to help me find out how many miles Fred lived from school. Numerous verbal battles ensued with the end result taking place at the dinner table one evening when Orville announced to Daddy, "Sis cannot learn," and I followed with, ". . . and he cannot teach." That ended that.

Finding myself upon a sea, adrift without a rudder, I remember telling God that night that I hated math. That it was dumb! Why was I required to learn something that wouldn't help me and that was going to keep me from being promoted to the next grade? For the most part, I was doing pretty well in school, but this subject was simply too hard. How was I going to be able to go to college some day, much less high school, if I didn't catch on to a subject in which I performed so poorly? Then I asked something like, "So would you help me, God—because Daddy doesn't have time and Orville doesn't know how?" After I had requested God's help, I remember the glimmer of a thought that I would never amount to anything if I didn't learn and that people whose life had a purpose or a meaning were those who had gone to school, had loved school, and had learned how to work through problems and find answers. Somehow I had the mistaken idea that learning, scholastic prowess, attending classes, being promoted, receiving a degree, were going to graduate me to a level of having "arrived"—that then, and only then, would I understand life and find reasons for everything that happened in it. In my childishness, I equated problems with solutions, learning with knowing, questions with answers, and I believed that once I was able to retain enough information to graduate, *then* I could quit learning because I would know it all and the knowing of it would automatically guarantee that my life amounted to something. Oh, the presumptions of youth!

My dad worked out a plan for Orville to spend a certain number of hours a week with me on word problems to encourage me and try to show patience in my primary area of academic struggle. Apparently Daddy also talked personally with Orville, because he seemed to be more understanding of my plight and cognizant of my genuine need for help as opposed to a sheer inability to learn. Instead of bossing me into comprehension, the reformed Orville would say, "Now think about this before you answer it, Sis. It's logical. Math is an exact science. Don't try to reason it out, and don't hurry, because if you think about it slowly, you can answer it correctly. I know you can." His kindness made me want to learn, if for no other reason than to please him because he said, "I know you can." For once he seemed to believe in me, and that alone reassured me about my person and my ability to learn.

I often studied in the school library, and while there one day, I opened my math book to get a beat on my after-school time with Orville, when my eye caught a sentence in the introduction. It read something like this: "Learning mathematics progresses civilization and helps man to have a better life."

"Good grief," I thought, "maybe there is some truth, after all, to needing this when I'm an adult. I'd better *really* think about the seriousness of these word problems." After that, mathematics didn't become any easier, but my attitude toward it changed. And at the end of the year I was promoted to seventh grade and to a whole new world of problems in junior high school.

As a brief aside, please permit me to quote an excerpt that I read many years later as I was contemplating the idea that one must do well in school and make high marks as a student before his or her adult life would be of benefit to others. It was written by Winston Churchill, and as I read it, I had to chuckle.

It was at "The Little Lodge" I was first menaced with Education. The approach of a sinister figure described as "the Governess" was announced. Her arrival was fixed for a certain day. In order to prepare for this day, Mrs. Everest [Churchill's nurse] produced a book called *Reading Without Tears*. It certainly did not justify its title in my case. I was made aware that before the Governess arrived I must be able to read without tears. We toiled each day. My nurse pointed with a pen at the different letters. I thought it was all very tiresome. Our preparations were by no means completed when the fateful hour struck and the Governess was due to arrive. I did what so many oppressed people have done in similar circumstances: I took to the woods . . . hours passed before I was retrieved and handed over to "the Governess." We continued to toil every day, not only at letters but at words, and also what was much worse, figures. Letters after all had only got to be known, and when they stood together in a certain way, one recognized their formation and that it meant a certain sound or word which one uttered when pressed sufficiently. But the figures were tied into all sorts of tangles and did things to one another which it was extremely difficult to forecast with complete accuracy. You had to say what they did each time they were tied up together, and the Governess apparently attached enormous importance to the answer being exact.

If it was not right it was wrong. It was not any use being "nearly right." In some cases these figures got into debt with one another: You had to borrow one or carry one, and afterwards you had to pay back the one you had borrowed. These complications cast a steadily gathering shadow over my daily life. They took one away from all the interesting things one wanted to do in the nursery or in the garden . . . they became a general worry and preoccupation. More especially was this true when we descended into a dismal bog called "sums." There appeared to be no limit to these. When one sum was done, there was always another. Just as soon as I managed to tackle a particular class of these afflictions, some other much more variegated type was thrust upon me.[1]

I found understandable comfort in that account, which turned out to be only the beginning of the revelation that some of the brightest, most clever minds that have emerged upon the horizon of history hated school. One of my Mentors, Hermann Hesse, said, "In me, school destroyed a great deal, and I know of few men of any stature who cannot say the same. All I learned there was Latin and lying."

It's a curious thing, but notwithstanding the fact that all phases of math were a thorn in my flesh, I loved school. There was something about the order of it that I found appealing and satisfying, and I always took an active interest in the schools I attended, from the lower grades through college. My brothers, too. We were involved with the music programs, sports, forensics, as well as learning precise skills and academics. And the level of my scholastic interest only deepened as I advanced in grades. It would never have occurred to me, for instance, as a college student, to revolt against the homilies by which the school was run.

---

1. *A Man of Destiny*, Winston Churchill (New York: Country Beautiful Foundation, Inc., 1965), p. 17.

But looking back, I believe the reason for that was not so much the fact that I lacked a rebellious spirit but rather this aforementioned overriding misconception that I was going to be all-knowledgeable upon graduation. College graduation day became a consuming goal. And what is even more curious is that on two highly emotional occasions my mother removed me from continuing college studies because she thought I was being negatively influenced by certain peers. I fought with her, verbally, tooth and nail, to be able to return to school to achieve my sought-after prize one day—a college diploma—and each time she reluctantly consented to let me return. This repeated dropping and reinstatement of courses took its toll in the time frame in which one generally finishes college. Consequently my degree plan took five years instead of four, with a change in majors twice. But God had set his plan in motion much earlier, and he was using all of these difficult adventures to teach me the lessons that proved to be the most vital part of my learning experience.

From a purely analytical point of view, I have tried to determine what it was about academia that gave me such delight. As I was idealistic by nature, I suppose it was a prescribed way of learning that was predictable, organized, skillful, and protected—an environment in which I felt safe from the onslaughts of life, while inwardly advancing in my own. I liked that feeling. College had an atmosphere of respect for authority, reverence for beauty, and attainable goals in view that Real Life did not seem to offer. One felt safe there, or I should be more accurate and say *I* felt safe, because it afforded me an environment for which my naive spirit longed, and it lifted me out of the milieu of unrest which I often experienced in clashing temperament with my mother. It provided the solace and order my psyche needed, and the learning experience itself was a lot of fun.

I remember one occasion in the classroom that has amused me privately for years. Being an art major required two years of Art History, a course I dearly loved. We studied famous paintings, all the great artists and their lives, as well as different periods of architecture and sculpture. It was a wonderful course which consistently moved my spirit. Our tests in those classes were generally made up of slides being flashed on a screen for two or three minutes each, while all the students madly wrote down the name of the painting and artist, the year it was completed, the epoch it represented, and anything else we could think of about that particular masterpiece. The idea was to be as accurate and detailed as possible in the few minutes the slide remained on the screen.

On this particular day we were having an Art History exam covering Italian paintings from the early Renaissance. One of the questions was to name the painting, the artist, year, and medium of that very famous work by Sandro Botticelli, *The Birth of Venus*, as a slide of it was being flashed on the screen in front of us. I kept staring at it but for the life of me, although I knew it well, I could not recall its name. I remembered the artist, the year, and even the medium, but the name? I was blank. Maybe you know that masterpiece—the nude goddess, Venus, with long blond hair, is the central figure, standing on an open seashell as it is being blown across the water to shore by two zephyrs. At the right of Venus is a nymph, hurrying with a mantle to meet her. It is a beautiful painting, and a marvelous study in graceful lines and patterns.

Finally, in desperation and out of time, I wrote down a nickname I had often called that painting during my study time (knowing full well it was wrong): *Venus on the Halfshell.* Would you believe my instructor either let me get by with that or never caught my mistake? And that was the only time in that entire course I made an A+ on a test. I was elated and I knew my secret was safe with Venus, who'd never tell.

Many years later, removed from that experience and college campus, I was visiting the Uffizi Gallery in Florence, Italy, where Botticelli's original hangs. I stood in front of it with two friends, an American and an Italian. Momentarily I forgot myself and muttered to the painting, "Well, there you are, old girl: Venus on the Halfshell." My friends looked at me and were very quick with their corrections. "No. That's *The Birth of Venus.*"

"I know. I know."

But back to the point I want to make as I think back upon my college years: In my passionate determination for an education and in my desire for an idealistic atmosphere in which to make decisions and live my life, upon graduation I was not prepared for anything, generally speaking, but school. The ideas of having to make a transition into real living and that education was nothing more than a set of tools to be used in knowing how to live (and never an end in itself) came as a tremendous shock to my whole person. I had duped myself into believing that school was going to tell me what my purpose was in life; that in its hallowed halls I would learn the answers to life's ceaseless questions and that later I would be able to solve each one as it arose in my life. It had never occurred to me that the value of education, like all striving for perfection, carries its purpose within itself.

It wasn't until I was the proud possessor of that much-sought-after sheepskin, and well into my own daily duties, that I realized all I really had from school was a handful of theories with which to work. For the first time, as I thought about all those years of striving for physical prowess, mental dexterity, or artistic beauty, what I had gained was in terms of its own reward. I wasn't any richer. I wasn't any more powerful. I wasn't any more beautiful or famous. I was still me!

Being one who wanted to pursue a career upon graduation (rather than marry a rich man, stay at home, lie in my hammock, and eat bon-bons), throughout my four or five years of college I kept thinking that at the moment I left campus, my career path would be pristine clear. I would no longer wonder, "Do I want to teach? Do I want to paint? Do I want to go for a master's?" Because I would know.

But I didn't know. I wasn't absolutely positive because life always held so many variables. Even as recently as 1976, I made a career change (within the same company) and in so doing I left the field of art behind me . . . that field for which I had studied so many years. At that recent a juncture in my life I once again questioned within myself, "Is this what I want to do with my life? Do I really want to go down this road? Can I be happy making this change?"

I also became aware when I finished college that my scholastic purpose lay in something almost indefinable—a life-feeling, a self-confidence. What had, at times, been an arduous journey of the improvement of the mind toward a definite goal was in fact nothing more than the broadening of my consciousness and the enriching of my possibilities for life and happiness. My goal, now achieved, proved to be only a stopping place to rest, not an end in itself. My formal education was only the beginning of a lifetime of learning. If I was indeed going to know the purpose for my life so that I could engage in action according to that purpose, it was not necessarily going to be by the enhancement of certain academic abilities. Rather it was going to lie in the extent of my involvement with God's purposes—using my gifts, as they had begun to be academically developed, in helping to solve the problems of the universe and in trying to understand and alleviate the needs of people.

My academic goal has been accomplished. But instead of a diploma, I've been handed a set of principles. By means of them, I find I am now unconsciously writing my own word problems. For example:

> Luci was born in 1932 and is now over fifty. The first twenty-five years of her life were spent in acquiring principles for living. The next twenty-five were spent in applying what she's learned. Which of the two periods has had the greater value?

OPERA

*The great artist looks beneath the flux of everyday
reality and sees eternal, unchanging symbols.
Behind the spasmodic, frequently inconsistent
activities of living men, he plainly
distinguishes the great currents which sweep
away the human soul.*

The article in the newspaper covered only a 3¼" x 1¾"
space, and it read easily enough, but when I followed
up on it, exhibited my courage, and took the risk, I
found that I had unwittingly walked through one of
the most exciting and challenging doors of my lifetime. It led to
fifteen years of disciplined commitment and an international
world of beauty, adventure, travel, and knowledge. I met people I
could never have met any other way. I participated in productions of enormous magnitude. I changed personalities and occupations at the drop of a hat. I hobnobbed in enviable circles. I
conversed and sang in other languages. Actually, I was no longer
walking on the earth: I was floating on a cloud. The article,
simple in its announcement, had a heading, twenty-one lines of
type, and looked like this:

Opera Auditions
Dallas Civic Opera will hold chorus auditions May
29 and 30 at Maple Theater for its 1959 season at
State Fair Music Hall. The company will give three productions November 6, 8, 12, 14, 19 and 21. Projected
are "Medea" and "Lucia di Lammermoor" with Maria
Callas and a third production to be selected, with "Il

Trovatore," "La Fille du Regiment" and "Tosca" likely prospects.

Assisting Lawrence Kelly with chorus auditions will be Margaret Hillis, founder/director of American Concert Choir and choral director for Santa Fe Opera. Miss Hillis will arrive from Chicago May 29 en route to Santa Fe.

I read and re-read the article, thinking, "Should I? Should I not?" You know how you do: You think of two reasons why you should follow up on such an idea, and fifteen reasons why you should not. I looked at the words *opera, productions, chorus,* and *Maria Callas* and thought, "Go for it!" But at the word *auditions,* I hurriedly changed my mind. I got scared. But I am a risk-taker by nature and one who loves a challenge, so my fears eventually subsided, at least long enough for me to start preparing the only operatic aria I knew, and I followed my first desire of "Go for it!"

Five years earlier, just prior to graduation from college, I had given a senior voice recital. One of the numbers on it was a mezzo-soprano aria entitled, "Voce di donna," from *La Gioconda,* by Amilcare Ponchielli. It was a song I had loved singing and one that, while not excessively demanding, showed off the voice to some degree . . . the type of vehicle I needed to demonstrate to an auditioning committee that I might possibly be one of the contraltos for whom they were looking. Up until that moment, my total exposure to opera had been singing that singular aria in a senior recital and attending a Metropolitan Opera performance of *Carmen* in Houston three years before. A friend had bought front row tickets for my mother and me, and upon seeing the opera, being close to Dimitri Metropolis as he conducted, and hearing that gorgeous, rich music—both vocally and orchestrally—I honestly thought I had died and gone to heaven. Nevertheless, by any stretch of the imagination, one could hardly call those two acquaintances an extensive exposure to opera.

However, fortified with several days of practice, the Swindoll maxim of "if anybody else can do it, you can do it too," and hours of prayer, I started out for the Maple Theater on May 29. That one moment of risk and courage set into motion a whole stream of events which caused me to gain a new respect for this couplet of Goethe:

> Whatever you can do, or dream you can, begin it.
> Boldness has genius, power, and magic in it.

About a week after that audition, I was notified I had been accepted as a chorister, and from that phone call on, the "genius, power, and magic" of opera began. I cannot find three words which better describe that particular art form, and I have seen each of the words used repeatedly in opera advertising. They truly capture the essence of it, both as a viewer and as a participant. In fact, permit me to steal that thought from Goethe as I look in retrospect at the unique and beautiful qualities of opera in its numerous parts and counterparts.

The Genius

Many people cannot stand opera. The very idea of attending one bores them into a coma. They do not understand its charm. They complain that opera productions are not sung in "their language" (whatever that may be), and the plots are too involved, irrational, or tedious. Kenneth Clark, one of my Mentors, you'll remember, had some of those same thoughts. He said:

> Opera, next to Gothic architecture, is one of the strangest inventions of western man . . . what on earth has given opera its prestige in western civilization—a prestige that has outlasted so many different fashions and ways of thought? Why are people prepared to sit silently for three hours listening to a performance of which they do not understand a word and of which they very seldom know the plot? Why do quite small towns all over Germany and Italy still devote a large portion of their budgets to this irrational entertainment?[1]

---

1. Kenneth Clark, *Civilisation, A Personal View* (New York: Harper & Row, 1969), pp. 241, 243.

Those are commonly asked questions; I used to ask some of them myself until I saw my first *Carmen*, and more specifically, until I stood behind the footlights as a chorister.

To me, the genius of opera lies in the fact that all of it—every inch of it—is the product of natural ability that has been carefully trained. The principal singers, the orchestra, the chorus, the ballet, the set designers, the lighting people, the costume designers, the production managers, the stage directors—each person first of all has a natural, essential, God-given gift . . . an innate, original, and creative capacity to produce a sound, or a dance, or a visual effect that is unique unto them. That gift, then, having been trained and honed into a thing of beauty, is blended together with all the other parts of the company, and the final result is one large mass of genius.

Perhaps you've heard an opera buff say, "Tonight I'm going to see *La Boheme*. It'll be my sixth time to see it." And you're thinking, "Sixth time! You can't mean it. What can possibly be that exciting about seeing the same opera six times?" But no two performances are the same. When there is a different roster of singers and an orchestra unfamiliar to your ears, there's a different sound. When there's a new set designer, one can expect different visual effects. When you've not seen the ballet company perform before, the dancing will be different. But in every case you can be sure that the talent which is displayed is born out of each individual's creative powers, both on the stage and backstage. Let me give you an example from my own opera experience.

The first stage director I had during my years in opera was Franco Zeffirelli. Franco, by all standards of measurement, is a genius. Not only do I read about his abilities in the newspaper almost daily nowadays, view the outpouring of his creative talents on the movie screen in the numerous films he produces and directs, but I have experienced his genius firsthand, having been under his direction myself. Of the thirty-two different operas in which I participated during my fifteen years as a Dallas Opera chorister, Franco directed nine of them. Such a brilliant man.

I've been in many technical rehearsals onstage with a group

of eighty plus choristers, a ballet troupe of ten or twelve people, five or six principal singers (of different nationalities), and have stood in awe as Franco has squinted his eyes as though he is carefully sizing up this band of unrelated individuals, and in only a matter of moments, seemingly, he has placed everybody where he wants them for that scene, all the while flitting from one language to another, speaking to each person in his or her own tongue. If that isn't genius, what is?

One of my most prized possessions from my opera career, in fact, is a score of *Lucia di Lammermoor*, the front flyleaf of which is covered with signatures of people with whom I worked that first year. Some of them are dead now: Maria Callas, Ettore Bastianini, Lawrence Kelly. But up in the left-hand corner is a note from Franco which reads, "Thank you! Friendship and . . . love! Franco Zeffirelli." I thought of that private note to me as I was watching his magnificent film, *La Traviata*, which came out this year. Another beautiful example of his genius! Franco Zeffirelli, who was born in the same town as Leonardo da Vinci, is the product of his early environment. His talents reflect a Renaissance and Shakespearian background and an understanding of the two, which have been interwoven into his volatile and colorful career. It seems that everything he touches turns into something that looks like a painting come to life, and working with him has made me have a tremendous respect for genius. Oh! And he is one of many.

Remember in chapter 7, "Mentors," where Kenneth Clark refers to genius near the end of his creed?

> Above all, I believe in the God-given genius of certain individuals, and I value a society that makes their existence possible.

I do, too. And I have loved being a part of not only a society, but an art form that values this genius in individuals.

While we're talking about the aspect of genius in the opera world, there were a number of individuals who made their American debuts in Dallas during the years I was a chorister. I had the happy and unique privilege of working with them onstage, and in some instances they came to my house for dinner or "after opera" parties, which started late and lasted till the wee hours of the morning. Those parties kept *everybody* awake. Even a "day person" like me. In particular, some of the more colorful individuals I recall and especially enjoyed were:

Franco Zeffirelli
Peter J. Hall
Bianca Berini
Luciana Novaro
Gilda Cruz-Romo
Magda Olivero
Roberto Benaglio
Norberto Mola

Dame Joan Sutherland and Placido Domingo also began their American careers in Dallas in 1961. I am extremely honored and count it a real joy to have been on the stage during those performances. And I remember very well what kind and friendly people they were. I should also mention how entranced I was with the flawless dancing of Margot Fonteyn, the artistic and sensitive baton of Nicola Rescigno, the incredible lighting of Tharon Musser, or the unique stage direction of Carlo Maestrini, Ellis Rabb, or John Houseman. And on. And on. Put them all together and they spell genius. That's what opera is all about. Or, is it . . .

The Power

I've often said if I had a nickel for every opera rehearsal hour I've attended, I could retire today. I would be a rich woman. (Well, maybe not rich, but certainly comfortable.) I have dragged my worn-out body to so many evening rehearsals, thinking I could not make it one more step, when within the first hour of singing, I've been revived by the sheer power of the music alone. Opera music is transporting and *gorgeous*. Not only are the more familiar arias worth remembering and singing in the shower or on the freeway, but some of the chorus music is unbelievably beautiful, too. I used to walk down the halls of the Mobil lab where I worked, singing the alto part to various opera choruses. Naturally, without a melody line, the music could be disconcerting to the listeners, but somehow the singing of it lifted me out of the milieu of my daily duties. It was as though I was transported out of my present surroundings.

I could give dozens of examples of this point from my opera days, but there is one which stands out in particular that I want to relate. Let me be somewhat esoteric for just a moment as I attempt to find the appropriate words to convey this event.

In 1960 the Dallas Civic Opera launched its first production of *Madama Butterfly*, an absolutely glorious piece of music by Puccini. I was among those chosen to be onstage as part of Butterfly's family (a small group of choristers). Naturally, I was thrilled to be in that company. The chorus music for *Madama Butterfly* is rich in harmony at some points and very simple in other spots, with the entire ensemble singing only the melody line. Probably its most famous choral interlude is what is known as the humming chorus, right at the end of Act II. The orchestra is playing a plaintive melody while the chorus (offstage) hums its sweeping phrases over that melody. Butterfly, her baby, and her maid, Suzuki, are the only ones onstage at the time, motionlessly waiting in the gathering darkness for the return of Lieutenant Pinkerton, Butterfly's husband. It's a very quiet, but highly emotional scene. And once again, the music is lovely.

One evening, prior to our usual rehearsal, I had been invited, along with Maestro Benaglio, my chorus master at the time (who didn't speak a word of English), to the home of some friends, Sandra and Roy Long. Sandra spoke fluent Italian, having lived in Italy before she married Roy. This particular evening she was preparing dinner, therefore spending most of her time in the kitchen, which left Roy and me in the living room with Maestro Benaglio. Roy spoke no Italian whatsoever, and I spoke only enough at that time to order spaghetti or linguini in an American restaurant . . . so together we all sat silently or conversed occasionally in varying stages of sign language.

After a bit, Maestro Benaglio got up from where he was sitting, walked over to an old rickety upright piano that Sandra and Roy owned (which was located near the chair in which I was sitting), lifted the lid off the keys, played a few random notes, then sat down on the piano bench. He slowly placed his hands on the keys and began to play softly the orchestral part to the *Butterfly* humming chorus. The piano was out of tune. A few keys were missing, but he didn't seem to notice, nor did he look up. He kept playing and when he came to the chorus part, he hummed. Oh, my friends . . . it was *beautiful.* Here was this master of choral music, who had conducted large groups of talented singers in Italy, Holland, Switzerland, France, and now in America; this man who had worked with the greatest voices in the world on television, in opera houses, on radio, for recordings; this individual who did not sing very well himself but knew every conceivable nuance of that music . . . playing and singing just for himself and us, lifting us right out of that living room because of the power of the music that Puccini had provided and that Benaglio had mastered. I wept. I could not help it and I will remember that simple occasion as long as I live.

Maestro Benaglio saw my tears and when he had finished the chorus, he put his hand on mine and said, "BEAUT-FUL, no?" Beautiful, indeed!

Every time I hear the humming chorus now, the only person I can see in my mind is a white-haired Italian gentleman seated at an old, broken-down piano, and I'm once again transported by the memory and power of that moment. That portion of *Madama Butterfly* will never be any more beautiful to me than it was that night.

This virtually unexplainable aspect of opera, this power that lies in the music, is one of its most engaging attributes. Perhaps you know what I mean from your own experience. If not with operatic music, then with other types of music. Have you ever been lifted out of depression or discouragement by singing or hearing the great hymns of the faith? Or called out of lethargy by listening to a magnificent symphony by Brahms, Beethoven, or Mahler? Felt patriotism as you've witnessed the American flag being raised to the playing of our national anthem? Or watched a baby fall sound asleep as his or her mother sang a soft, loving lullaby? If so, then you know what I mean.

I've experienced all of that, time and time again—the emotions that are evoked are a result of the power of the music. And guess what . . . the language in which any of those sounds are produced is really irrelevant. It's the music that's the vehicle for our feelings. The words, perhaps, may personalize a message, but the beauty, the universal appeal, the power lies in that artistic ability to combine vocal or instrumental sounds into melody, harmony, rhythm, arrangement, or timbre—what we commonly call music. Music "generates" the opera, and in that sense it goes back to the genius of the composer. There would be no opera without music and that's why those of us who are opera lovers attend every chance we get. The power of the music makes opera what it is. Or is it . . .

The Magic

In his autobiography, Hermann Hesse, another Mentor, tells us of his desire to write a magical opera:

> It was the ambition of my later life to write a sort of opera in which human life in its so-called reality would be viewed with scant seriousness, ridiculed, in fact; in its eternal value, however, it would shine forth as image and momentary vesture of the Godhead . . . to express these thoughts or attitudes toward life seemed to me possible only by means of fairy tales, and I looked upon the opera as the highest form of fairy tale. In my opera I wanted to do what I had never quite succeeded in doing in my poetry: to establish a high and delightful meaning for human life. I wanted to praise the innocence and exhaustibility of nature and to present her course up to that point where, through inevitable suffering, she is forced to turn toward spirit, her distant polar opposite, and the oscillation of life between these two poles of nature and of spirit would be revealed as blithe, playful, and complete as the arch of a rainbow.[2]

---

2. Hermann Hesse, *Autobiographical Writings* (New York: Farrar, Straus and Giroux, 1972), pp. 58-59.

That's an interesting mouthful, isn't it? It's so profound, it sounds somewhat like scripture, especially that part about "inevitable suffering" or the "two poles of nature and of spirit." (Reminds me of the time I was reading a short paragraph out of a volume entitled *The Music of Man*, by Yehudi Menuhin, to my friend Winky Leinster. It was about music being the oldest form of expression, "older than language or art." Menuhin referred to the fact that "music touches our feelings more deeply than most words and makes us respond with our whole being . . . as long as the human race survives, music will be essential to us. We need music, I believe, as much as we need each other." When I finished reading that to Winky, who was listening very attentively, she said, "That's beautiful. Almost sounds like scripture—wonder if I could use it some way in my prayer time." I said, "Sure. Quote it to God. He'll love it . . . and he'll probably agree!")

One of the meanings of the word "magic" is "anything that has an extraordinary or irresistible influence." I can tell you that that is certainly true of opera. I'm not talking about magic in the occult sense. I'm talking about magic in the ocular sense— magic in the eye of the beholder.

The first time our company performed *Suor Angelica*, another Puccini opera, I had never seen such a set in my life. I honestly felt as though I was standing out-of-doors in the sun-drenched courtyard of a Tuscan convent. Viewing it from out front with proper lighting, of course, the effect was even more realistic and beautiful. When we performed *Otello*, I could almost feel the heat from a fire scene—all accomplished with lights and fans. And *Macbeth?* Oh, *Macbeth*—now there's an opera for you. In the spring before our fall production of it with the Dallas Opera, I had seen *Macbeth* in West Berlin on a massive stage, and I thought at one point all the chorus would never get onstage. They came and came and kept coming. Then, finally, when the last one arrived, they sang together about the oppression of their country, "Patria opressa"—a lovely, harmonious outcry of the human heart which longs to be free. In Italian, German, or English—in *any* language, that emotion is the same, and the visual effect is one of magic, conveyed on the wings of music.

I have a photo album of all my years with the opera which I have entitled, "Ah! This Is Opera!" and every now and then I pull it off the shelf, look through it, and recreate for myself a nostalgic fairy tale. During those years of performing I changed occupations, hair color, and nationalities faster than the speed of light. I was a school teacher, a nun, a courtesan, a cigarette salesgirl, a member of a royal family, a witch, a party goer, a peasant, a prisoner, and a slave; with red hair, black hair, blonde hair, gray hair, and no hair. My ancestry was French, Italian, Turkish, Greek, German, Spanish, Scottish, Hebrew, and Japanese. If that ability is not a feat of magic, then what should I call it?

Then, finally, opera is downright fun. It's the esprit de corps among all the show people. You've worked hard for weeks and months, attending rehearsals, memorizing music, blocking out staging, fitting costumes, trying on wigs, staying late, coming early . . . then "suddenly" one night—Bang! The curtain goes up, the orchestra is playing full tilt, the lights are in your eyes, and there you are—in performance. There's nothing quite like it. For three-and-one-half hours or so you are transported into another world and another time in history. You are somebody else, bringing genius, power, and magic to an entire audience of rapt individuals, many of whom are no doubt looking at you, thinking, "Boy, that looks fun. Wonder how all those people ever got into that? They make it look so easy. I think I'll investigate being in opera." So the beat goes on . . .

There are so many things I could have said in this chapter.

In fact, I started to call it "Music" instead of "Opera" because of my inordinate love of music in general. But as I thought about it and reviewed in my mind the profound effect that the world of opera—that particular art form alone—has had upon me personally, I decided to limit the chapter to opera. There was so much to relate in that field without touching any of the other areas of music I thoroughly enjoy.

Fifteen years of singing with an opera company creates an

enormous platform for fascinating memories. I could have drawn for you one funny verbal picture after another that left me in stitches, such as the time a red balloon from the second act of *La Boheme* (which had escaped into the rafters on a Friday night performance) fell squeakingly onto the stage during the big love scene in *Thais* the following Saturday night. I could have told of the many times I was unable to sing in a performance because my heart was so moved by the sheer beauty of it all, as in the sextet in *Lucia* that first year, while I attempted to be vocal and articulate while standing only two or three feet from Maria Callas. Or I could have elaborated on the many "after-opera" parties mentioned earlier that my roommate and I gave at our apartment, and the joy of having all those expressive Italians in our home, visiting, talking, eating, joking—especially the night Luciana Novaro (once prima ballerina at La Scala) danced the tarantella on my coffee table to the music of our record player. I could go on and on and on . . . but there's simply not time, and that's not my primary point.

What I've tried to do in this chapter is to show that the deepest qualities of opera are unchanging symbols, symbols that are true of all greatness, especially in various fields of art. It is so easy to get caught up in the moodiness and petty inconsistencies of artistic humanity that we miss this deep and eternal mark of beauty. What makes any art great is that it has consistent symbols, and these symbols of greatness carry it from century to century in spite of the temperamental behaviors of the individuals who generate it or the flux of everyday realities. Perhaps that is the answer to Kenneth Clark's query: "What on earth has given opera its prestige in western civilization—a prestige that has outlasted so many different fashions and ways of thought?"

It's genius, power, and magic. I know. I've seen it happen. And better still, I've been part of the fairy tale that made it happen.

PROJECTS

*I believe that one of man's most legitimate pleasures
is to toil and see his toil bearing fruit . . . for,
by believing passionately in something which still
does not exist, we create it. The nonexistent is
whatever we have not sufficiently desired,
whatever we have not irrigated with our blood to
such a degree that it becomes strong enough to
stride across the somber threshold of non-existence.*

I n the fall of 1979 I received a letter from Sophia Stylianidou, my Greek friend who lives in Athens, and with whom I had regularly corresponded for nine years at that time. Except for one thing, the letter was not any different from most I had received from her throughout the years. It was well-expressed, loving, informative, and clever. The factor that made this letter different, however, was an enclosure and a few paragraphs written near the end. The enclosure was a photocopy of a doctor's prescription, and the closing paragraphs of the letter told me of a young man, the cousin of the lady for whom Sophia worked, who was becoming paralyzed and was in need of a particular drug. The cousin (a man whom I had not met and whose name I had not been told) had been examined by doctors in both Greece and Rumania, who ultimately prescribed a medication called "Utiplex," which (according to the Rumanian doctor) could only be found in America. The prescription was dated August 10, 1979, and Sophia's letter was written September 23. The name of the drug itself had been circled and the prescription was written in both Rumanian and Latin. Since it was found only in America, Sophia asked if I could get the drug for Irene, her supervisor, and mail it to their place of business. Then she closed her letter with this brief paragraph:

> I am sorry I am giving you so much trouble, but it's a matter of health, and somebody's life is depending on this special medicine.

Immediately my mental wheels went into motion. When I read the letter and studied the prescription, along with her request, I realized the need was imminent. I got up and drove to a nearby drugstore which I often frequent and where the druggist and I know one another by name. I told him Sophia's story, gave him the prescription, asked if I could wait for it to be filled, and envisioned myself leaving momentarily with vial in hand, heading straight for the post office. But I was in for a surprise. After listening carefully, studying the prescription, and making a few phone calls, the druggist turned to me and said, "Luci, there is no way you can send medicine to Greece. It is not legal to mail drugs across international waters. You'll have to find some other method for your friends to get help. I'm sorry."

Disappointed, but far from defeated, I drove home praying, "Well, Lord, what now? Here these people are in tremendous need, and I've got the key in my hand to unlock this dilemma for them, but I've just been told I can't mail medicine to Greece. Will you please help me think of a creative alternative? And fast, God . . . because it sounds like this guy's time is running out. Give me an idea."

Pulling up in front of my house, I found myself deep in thought about this challenge. I racked my brain for an idea. Nothing came. When I arrived inside I made my own phone calls to several pharmaceutical businesses in the area. Nothing. They had not heard of Utiplex and were all very vague as to my acquiring it under the related circumstances. That was out. I was facing a blank wall . . . I could almost see it in front of me, and I remember consciously thinking, with my hand on the telephone, "God . . . please write on that blank wall. You did it for people in the Old Testament. Will you do it for me? Help me know what to do. Irene and Sophia are depending on me." I felt a bit like King Arthur looking for the Holy Grail. The object of my search was out there somewhere, but how was I going to find it?

The next day, I decided to write Kay Kosinski, a Christian friend who had, at an earlier time, met Sophia and who was employed as an administrator in the health care field at a large hospital in Austin, Texas. In fact, not only was Kay medically knowledgeable, but I knew her to be an extremely attentive and tender person, willing to go to whatever means necessary in helping others, as well as one who thrived on challenges. I sent her the prescription and carefully explained the situation, plus its urgency. True to Kay's unselfish nature, she instantly took up the challenge and went to work on it. She inquired into who made the drug and for what disease it was prescribed. She conducted extensive research, calling on others in the profession to assist her, and while waiting on their responses, she discovered that the young man in question had what is commonly called "Lou Gehrig's Disease," or ALS (amyotrophic lateral sclerosis). She learned that it was progressive and degenerative and that even with proper medication, there was little hope of recovery. Nevertheless, her persistence and loving availability proved to be God's answer to my prayer.

After days of research, correspondence, phone calls, and tireless effort in many directions, Kay found out that Utiplex was manufactured only in England. She wrote to the ALS Foundation in New York and requested they send all available literature on the subject to our friend in Athens. She also wrote a detailed letter to me, telling me of her findings, as well as of the importance of keeping faith in dealing with the disease, and promising prayer for the young man who had it, but whom neither of us knew. Upon receiving Kay's letter, I wrote Sophia with a full report of Kay's findings, and our mutual delight in being able to help her and her friends.

On October 25, Sophia answered my letter, and these were her three opening paragraphs:

How can I start this letter without tears coming into my eyes? Just a "thank you," I am afraid, is not enough. I feel a bit guilty, because in asking for the medicine, I am sure I gave you so *much* trouble. Not only to you, but to Kay as well. You have both spent so much effort. Thank you. Thank you, from the bottom of my heart.

. . . Irene is thanking you very much for everything you have done! We could never imagine that from a simple, friendly letter, there would be moved a whole machinery of events—from Greece to California, from California to Texas, from Texas to New York, from New York to England, from England back to Greece—It's great! And, it's amazing how people can help if they want to. The world becomes so small, without frontiers, without hatred and passions. It's wonderful. I wish it were so, all the time.

Right now, we have in our hands lots of information from the ALS Foundation (who have written to me directly), and they are asking me to let them know if I need any more information or help about this disease. I will write them as soon as we are ready.

On November 26 she wrote again. "Irene visited London and got the medicine. Her cousin is much improved . . . he has to take the medicine the rest of his life. She asked me to thank you again. She is extremely excited and I am very moved because of your generosity in helping us. I know how you feel about people. I feel the same. That's why we are friends."

The reason I have gone into such detail in the aboverelated story is because *that* is what I mean by a project! Webster defines project as "a proposal of something to be done; an act or a plan of action; a design in which something is carried out." I honestly believe that engaging in projects—either alone or with the assistance of others, as demonstrated in this account—has done as much as, if not more than, any other singular activity in my life to teach me the precepts of scripture and the commandments of God. When one decides that he or she is going to get involved in an endeavor, either alone or with others, at that moment of action one is inviting God to chip away at the process of character building. One is walking into God's furnace of fire.

Let's take the writing of this book as an example. The moment I alone said yes to such a commitment, the same series of rules and measurements went into play as was exhibited in the "medicine story" with Sophia and Kay. A very clear-cut order of activities began: I had to have a desire to write the book. I needed a goal in mind in terms of completion, both to tell my publishers and to plan anything else in life. In other words, if I meant business, my goal had to be realistic—not too soon, but not so far away that I would still be working on the book ten years from now. I had to recognize there would be times I could see no light at the end of the tunnel; times I wanted to throw in the towel and say, "I quit!" And during those hours, I needed to learn patience with myself and my circumstances. Writing a book (living in and through it for a certain number of months), then seeing it come to actual publication would build my confidence in myself. Whether or not it was a smashing success or the world's biggest flop was *really* not the basic issue. The basic issue was seeing it through to the end. All that, and more, goes into a project and it's during those hours of heat and trial that the mettle is tested, the dross is sifted out, the character is refined, and that which was once only a thought "strides across the somber threshold of non-existence."

Look for a moment at the steps in a project: In 1 Corinthians 14:40, we are encouraged to do everything "properly, in a good and orderly way." The accomplishment of any project first begins with order, an organization of the facts, the conflicts, the means at hand, the desired results. It means thinking everything through first. It's what I call "The Studied Approach."

When I was in high school I decided to make my own Christmas cards one year. I dashed down to the art store, bought all the needed equipment for a linoleum block print—the piece of linoleum, x-acto knife, a brayer for rolling on the color, the ink, and paper for printing. The card was to have a simple design, and lettered beneath it, MERRY CHRISTMAS. That sounds easy enough, doesn't it? I drew it off on paper first, then transferred it to the block. After three or four evenings of cutting a linoleum relief with as steady a hand as possible, I was finally ready to print. You cannot know my disappointment when I lifted the block off that first print only to realize I couldn't read MERRY CHRIST-MAS because it was reversed, having carved it "readable" during all those evenings of working on it. To read correctly, the design had to be backward from what I wanted to print, and I hadn't realized this because of my haste in getting on with the job.

Haste has ruined many a project for me in my early years of being a "do-it-yourselfer." But after enough of those times, one comes to realize that planning is one of the most vital, foundational elements in getting anything accomplished. I'm not negating spontaneity at all, please understand. On the contrary, I love spontaneous, spur-of-the-moment events; but in the long-range projects they really have no place. Organization, however, is a skill, and all skills can be improved upon. So I'm saying when we learn to organize in one or two areas, the same principles apply to all areas where organization is beneficial and required, and the result is organizational proficiency. The converse is also true: If we never start, we'll never learn.

The second valuable commodity that is refined out of the furnace of a project is patience. The most patient individuals I know personally almost always enjoy projects. When one is engaged in an undertaking which requires any investment of time at all, one frequently has only two choices—give up or be patient. In Romans 5:3 and 4, there is reference to this desirable quality of patience.

> We can rejoice, too, when we run into problems and trials for we know that they are good for us—they help us learn to be patient. And patience develops strength of character in us and helps us trust God more each time we use it until finally our hope and faith are strong and steady.

Ever try to lose weight? What does it take more than anything else? Patience. Ever had to recover from surgery? What is the primary requirement for one's attitude? Patience. Ever wanted to build up a savings account? What is needed during the long haul? Patience.

Patience is never acquired from reading about it in a book or observing it in the lives of others. It is the fruit of difficulty and the by-product of learning how to wait. I think it is one of life's hardest lessons, and one of the best ways to learn it is to voluntarily involve ourselves in projects.

Up the road from where I live, two fellas are building a house. They have done virtually all the work themselves. Day after day after day they are there, slaving over that project together, pouring their energies into it. They've been working on it for about a year and a half and are two-thirds through, I would imagine. The other evening I was taking a walk, and as I was going by that place, once again noticing their progress, I saw the two of them standing on a pile of discarded lumber, looking appraisingly at their nearly-completed project. I only caught a portion of their conversation as I approached them. Apparently they were trying to decide what to name their masterpiece. Just as I got even with them, one of them put both hands in the air, as though he were blessing the house, and said, "Patience. Let's name it Patience. We've put more of that into it than anything else."

I knew exactly how they felt. I've labored over a project for hours, days, and weeks, and thought as I was hammering the last nail or staining the last board or painting the last wall or printing the last letter—"Well, finally! If this thing had a name, it would have to be Patience. Because I've given it all I've got."

I have two friends with whom I am constantly working on projects. We've spent evenings, weekends, or portions of our vacations together, building memories in that manner. Projects are a very real part of our relationship, and together we've tackled some real whoppers! Building a fence. Making picture frames. Developing film. Refinishing furniture. Planting a garden. Giving each other a haircut. Cleaning carpets. Baking bread. (I always thought it would be fun to write a book about that project, since I found baking bread to be a rather difficult task. I could entitle it, *One Loaf, That's All I Knead.*) Choosing and buying a cat. Weaving a rug. Making pasta. Installing an air conditioner. Defrosting a refrigerator. Hanging drapes. Roofing a house.

You name it—we've done it, I do believe. And in *every* case, patience was the ingredient most needed to bring the project to conclusion. Stick-to-it-ive-ness! That's what it takes, gang, and that's the commodity that separates the winners from the losers. There's no better way in the world to build patience than to throw our energies into a task that lies ahead of us.

Amazingly enough, however, the more patience we spend, the more we regain. It's like a boomerang. We send it out and back it comes, to be sent out again.

Projects also build confidence. Since Kay and I were able to aid our Greek friend in her request, we have said to ourselves, and between ourselves, "We can do it again. Lay it on us!" And I have noticed the more patience one learns to exhibit, the greater the opportunity to build confidence. By that I mean you see a problem and you tackle it, head on. In it your abilities are tested but you don't give up. You hang in there and your patience grows. Finally you work through the problem. Then you say to yourself, "Well, that was tough. But it wasn't impossible. I might even do it again." Thus confidence grows. The apostle James says it this way, in chapter 1, verses 3 and 4:

> When the way is rough, your patience has a chance to grow. So let it grow, and don't try to squirm out of your problems. For when your patience is finally in full bloom, then you will be ready for anything, strong in character, full and complete.

Confidence helps us have "staying power." Because we know we will learn valuable lessons from our tests, we hang in there. Confidence is assurance and the having of it makes us "ready for anything, strong in character, full and complete." Who doesn't want to feel that?

Finally, the end result of a project is celebration. There is nothing quite like being through with something and sensing accomplishment. It is a wonderful emotion, and if the project was conducted by several people, the celebration builds unity among them. Collectively, you have the feeling of, "We did it. We *really* did it. Let's celebrate!" And . . . you definitely should. That's my favorite part of a project.

Four building blocks: plans, patience, confidence, celebration. That's the whole package in a nutshell, and it's a process that must go in that order. Each part grows out of the one before it and none is more valuable or less valuable than the others.

We must also remember that all the while we are building something outside of ourselves, we are at the same time building something within. It's called character. My only regret about that project is the fact that when it's completed, I'll be too old to celebrate.

WORK

The times through which we are passing . . . are difficult ones. Difficulty, however, has always been life's stimulant, awakening and goading all our impulses, both good and bad, in order to make us overleap the obstacle which has suddenly risen before us. Thus we sometimes reach a point much further than we had hoped: by mobilizing all our forces, which otherwise would have remained asleep or acted reluctantly and without concentration.

What a coincidence! Exactly twenty-five years ago on the date I am writing this, August 25, 1983, I walked into my job at Mobil Oil Corporation for the very first time, and I've been "mobilizing all my forces" ever since. (I couldn't resist!) Even though I was a greenhorn in a hundred different ways when I was twenty-five, there was one thing I was fairly sure of. I had been out of college for three years, working at various jobs during that time, but always with the hope in the back of my mind of returning to school to work on a master's degree. Fact is, when I was being considered for my job with Mobil, one of the men who interviewed me, Stan Wilhelm, said, "Do you plan to work here for a year and then get married and leave us?"

To which I replied, "Sir, I plan to work for a year, then hopefully go back to school for a master's degree. And I don't ever plan to get married."

Completely ignoring my prophetic prediction about leaving

to go to school, he replied, "Oh, you don't ever plan to get married? Why not? Most girls who are single and your age work for a year, then quit to get married. That costs Mobil a lot of money to train them, only to have them quit. How can you be so sure you won't get married?"

To which I launched into a short speech on one of my goals from childhood: "Mr. Wilhelm," I said, "all my life I have loved the idea of a career. Since I was about ten or twelve years old, I decided I didn't want to marry. I can't really tell you why except that a career, as opposed to marriage, holds more appeal for me, and I don't believe I personally could successfully handle both. Therefore, with the exception of more schooling, I would like to have a career with Mobil, if Mobil likes me and I like it."

With a studied look at my face while I was talking, Mr. Wilhelm listened very intently. Then when I had finished he said, "That will be all." After a couple of seconds, I got up, walked to the door, and was thinking, "All what? . . . All there is to the interview? All there is to my future with Mobil? All there is to my ideas about marriage vs. career? All what?" At the doorway I glanced back at him and he was smiling. Then he said, "Thank you," and that was it. About a week later I was called to report to work on a Monday, August 25, 1958, and I've been reporting there every Monday since. Never left to work on a master's degree . . . and never got married. (I was right in at least one of my comments during that initial interview.)

When I started to work for Mobil Oil Corporation, it was love at first sight. And looking at it now from a twenty-five-year backward glance, let me hasten to add I am *so* glad I never left. Mobil is a wonderful company and I can and do easily and readily sing its praises. I believe of all the many benefits that have been mine as a result of working with Mobil, one of the very best has been the sense of esprit de corps in a cooperative setting. Somehow from that first Monday I felt I "belonged." I never had the feeling, "Gosh, I've really got to 'prove' myself here, or they'll never accept me." From day one everybody was friendly to me—warm, caring, inclusive, and kind. With a few exceptions I felt I could be very natural in all situations, unlike many places of business where the moment the employee enters the front door of the office he or she puts on an "office personality"—becomes another person. I was introduced to everyone, invited to coffee breaks, invited to lunch—even included in "football pots" . . . which I have never really enjoyed or understood! How can I better express it? I felt I "belonged."

I like Mobil's progressiveness; I like its professionalism; I like the fact that in all its "bigness" it seems to care about people; I like how it permits me to do creative, constructive work and retain my own personhood and dignity. And for every one of those aspects I enjoy, I could cite an example from my own career experience—but most of all, I like the fact that it is a corporation that stands tall on togetherness, because that says to me that I don't personally have to know all the answers to all the problems. There are others who will help me if need be—work with me instead of against me—and from whom I can feel support and encouragement. To me, a company or a work place is only as good and successful as its people, and unless the people involved are able to depend on one another and seek to cooperate for the good of everyone, in time the entire structure will be undermined and its mission for being will not be accomplished. If we spend 40 hours a week at work, that's 2,000 hours per year. Who wants to devote that much time anywhere without feeling accepted and supported?

For sixteen of my twenty-five years with Mobil I worked in research in various stages of drafting and technical illustration. A research lab atmosphere is extremely creative and imaginative while being highly technical. Mobil has been in research since the day it was born. The company was, in fact, established to test a scientific hypothesis: that crude oil, distilled under a vacuum, would yield a greater portion of kerosene, a most valuable product needed in the early years of Mobil's history. Since that day, of course, Mobil's trademark is that of a tradition—forward-looking research and development.

By beginning my career in research, immediately I was surrounded by people who insisted on qualities and standards of excellence and who were continually aware of their responsibilities to the community of humanity. I liked that, too, because it kept me on my toes and it provided a personal incentive toward job satisfaction in the broadest sense of the word—that feeling of being engaged in important and rewarding work with a commitment to the betterment of people and their environment.

Remember in chapter 8, "School," where I talked about the realization that if I was ever going to know the purpose for my life it was not going to be by the enhancement of certain academic abilities? Rather, it was going to lie in helping to solve the problems of the universe and in trying to understand and alleviate the needs of people. Well . . . this was what I experienced when I went to work for Mobil Oil. It was in the research environment of Mobil I came to know that, for me, higher academic development was not going to aid me that much in the accomplishment of my overall purpose for living. My search for the answers to life's questions could be continued in that setting as successfully as in an academic environment . . . perhaps even more realistically. Therefore after a year in Mobil's research lab I no longer had the desire to begin a master's program. I was already on the cutting edge of life, I felt. (Sometimes I wish I had a master's— just for my own personal enhancement, but the ideal time to have acquired one was in the three-year period between graduation from college and entrance into research work. Now when I am asked to advise someone regarding a career or schooling, I tell them if they aim toward a degree higher than undergraduate, to begin pursuing it no later than one year after college graduation. Every year after that, the chances of acquiring one lessen.)

In the late 1960s Mobil's Research Laboratory in Dallas had the exciting privilege of being actively involved with NASA in the moon shot and moon walk. That occasion, particularly, revealed to me the constant and far-reaching possibilities of research which are not always known or planned at the outset of any undertaking. I remember many occasions when my colleague, Doris Fleeman (a dear friend and fine artist), and I worked long, hard, tedious hours on the preparation of numerous slides and graphic illustrations of technical data to aid in this project.

Often the work was difficult, with pre-set time frames in which to complete our tasks. But when the petroleum industry's only primary investigator of lunar samples, Dr. Bob Sippel, came from "our" lab, everybody's unified effort seemed worth it. Initially Dr. Sippel was conducting research on the luminescence properties of rocks in order to further Mobil's understanding of geologic processes in its search for petroleum, yet the final result of that technological study (or at least one of them) was his ability to make a valid and noteworthy contribution to NASA's gathering and studying of "moon rocks." Dr. Sippel and a colleague of his made color photographs of a lunar sample from Tranquility Base, as seen through a polarizing microscope. Those photographs were exhibited at the lab, and when I saw them for the first time, I remember that I almost felt like crying, I was so moved within. To think, I had had a part in that! My work, those long hours of slide preparation and the graphic illustrations I designed—added to a chain of people attempting to achieve the same results, with the final expertise of Bob Sippel—had made this happen. It was exciting, very exciting, and I don't remember so much thinking "I work for Mobil and I'm proud of it," as much as "I'm on a team, and we won. All right!"

In my research days we had occasion (for a recruiting brochure we were designing) to define "research" as we understood it, and together we came up with this: "Vital research doesn't just happen . . . it is the conscious balancing of man's love of knowledge with his real life requirements." I have thought about that definition a lot and now, many years removed from research, I can honestly say that I have learned from experience that *nothing* just happens, unless we don't care about the results. Everything in life takes a conscious balancing. God implanted the principle of that definition in my brain then, and I've been unconsciously using it ever since.

Three years before I left the research lab to transfer to the West Coast, my mother died very suddenly and unexpectedly. She passed away on a Tuesday evening, and her funeral was held two days later. In the register of those in attendance, forty-seven signatures are of friends from the Mobil Research Lab. I remember well that Mr. Wilhelm, the man who had hired me thirteen years earlier, told those who wanted to attend but had no transportation to get there, to go in company cars, and his was among the signatures of those who came. I believe that act of support on the part of my friends at the lab, if nothing else, locked me into Mobil for life.

Esprit de corps!

Not only does Mobil instill in me a group spirit that comes with unity, but strange as it seems it also does the opposite. Because I feel Mobil is behind me, supporting me and believing in me, that encourages me to stand alone . . . to be firm in my convictions without wavering, knowing what I say and do all by myself will be backed up by a whole army of employees. Let me explain what I'm saying because I believe that experiences where we have to stand alone aid so much in the overall maturing process. This is an illustration of something that occurred one rainy evening in February, 1979, after my transfer to the West Coast, three years into my "new" career as a Rights of Way Agent for Mobil, West Coast Pipe Lines Department.

Part of my responsibility as an agent for the Pipe Lines Department was to represent Mobil before various city councils and boards in the acquisition of franchises for use of city streets and rights of ways to install our pipeline. This particular duty involved writing letters to city attorneys, negotiating terms, conditions, and related costs for such privileges, and attending evening council meetings should I need to verbally clarify Mobil's standards and desires, as well as to answer any questions that might arise from a council member or a citizen. My training for this had come from my supervisor, Bill Collins, who had had thirty-six years with Mobil, was an excellent negotiator, and one who had vast experience in the various rights-of-way disciplines. But there's only so much any supervisor can do. Sooner or later the employee is on his or her own!

I arrived alone at the city council meeting that night, in Norwalk, California, a city in the Los Angeles basin where our company maintains four-and-one-half miles of pipeline, and I was introduced by the mayor as the representative from Mobil

Oil Corporation. He asked that I stand where I was in the audience, and answer questions which might arise regarding the renewal of our franchise. No questions were asked so I sat down and the council meeting went on to other issues. While I was on my feet, I had noticed a man across the aisle who watched me very intently as the mayor was introducing me and as I was awaiting questions. I paid him no real attention until I was ready to leave the meeting and turned to get a better look at him. His seat was empty and he was nowhere to be seen. It is customary for people in the audience to come and go at will when their particular item of business on the agenda has been discussed, so I assumed he had left the building to go home. Giving it little or no thought, I gathered up my purse, briefcase, raincoat, and I too walked out. It was about 9:00 P.M. and dark except for the few lights around the building.

Just as I walked out the door of the council chambers and had gone about ten feet, this man emerged from behind some bushes. He walked right up to me, stood very close to me, looked me straight in the eye, and said, "Are you the representative from Mobil Oil?" I told him that I was. He began cursing me with a string of vulgar words I could hardly believe. I said nothing . . . just stood there, listening to him, trying to believe my ears. The entire time he was cursing me, petroleum companies in general, and Mobil in particular, he was rolling up a newspaper very tightly in his hands as though he was going to club me with it or something.

But here's the amazing part: I wasn't afraid; not then anyway. Later, when I had time to think about what had happened, my knees were knocking, but at the moment he encountered me I was unusually composed. He cursed for probably a full minute (which seemed like an hour!), calling me filthy names—vomiting out all the garbage that was stored up in his soul. When there was finally a lull, I said, "How can I help you, sir?" and somehow I genuinely meant it. He informed me that he owned a trucking firm and was unable to get gas for his trucks; that he would soon be out of business if oil companies didn't lower their prices. I listened.

Then he said (and I put it mildly), "If I had a gun, I'd kill you right now. None of you oil company people are any damn good anyway." I continued to listen, so he went on. "All we do nowdays is wait in line for gas. Then when we get to the head of the line, either there isn't any more or we can't afford it. You're killin' us and somebody oughta' be killin' you. One of these days there's gonna be an uprising in this country against the oil companies and I'm gonna lead it and we're gonna wipe you off the face of the earth . . ." and he continued his invective.

After listening as attentively as I could, praying all the while, and trying to perceive his body language, as well as his *real* message, while he dumped out all his curse words, when I felt I had a clear picture of his predicament, I butted in. "Excuse me, but what is your name?" He told me his name. Then I said, "Do you have a business card? If so, may I have one please?" He backed away a bit, put down the paper he had been rolling up, took out his billfold, and handed me a business card from it. When I looked at it I saw the name of his trucking firm in the center of the card and his name in the left hand corner. His partner's name (in the lower right corner) had been scratched out. I figured he had killed him in a fit of anger probably, then marked his name off their business cards. As he handed me the card, he pointed out that he was president of that "outfit" and therefore carried a lot of weight. In other words, I heard him say in so many words, "Don't fool with me, sister!"

I looked at him. "Jim," I said, "I appreciate your telling me your problem. Really! Mobil cares a lot about just these kinds of concerns, and I'm going to give my supervisor your card and ask if there's anything we can do for you." He looked at me and the muscles in his face relaxed a little bit. I went on. "I know how you feel about waiting in line for gas. Today I waited over an hour, and when I got to the head of the line they were out of unleaded—at a Mobil station. I was just sick after all that waiting, but that is a condition that none of us seems to be able to control."

He said, "Aw, don't gimme that . . . you don't wait for gas." I assured him that I did and that in a gas war I was a casualty, too, just as he was. I pointed out how all of us were adversely affected by OPEC prices and that Mobil Oil Corporation didn't like it any better than he did. I asked him if he had a family, how many trucks he owned, how long he had been president of his company—a number of similar questions—and eventually he calmed down a great deal. He seemed surprised (and almost grateful, in a strange way) that I took time to listen to him, much less care about his problem and his life. It was a sad commentary on how the "little guy" thinks he is being swallowed up by the mighty power of corporate structure when the real truth is that often we are *all* victims of circumstances beyond our control and we must try to understand each other's dilemmas in order to cope in this world.

I would not say we parted friends. (In fact, as I was leaving, he yelled, "By the way, what's *your* name, lady?" "Swindoll," I said. "Luci Swindoll." "Swindle . . . well, that's a good name for you! It fits! You drive careful now, ya' hear!" What irony!) But we didn't part enemies either. On the way home, I felt weak, and as I thought about how close I came to being beaten up or killed, perhaps—*then* I was nervous. Nevertheless, I was glad I had listened to him because it helped me understand the very real problems people face as they view oil companies.

The next day I called Mobil's marketing department to see if there was anything we could do to help Jim and his trucking firm. There wasn't, because of the price conditions set by both OPEC and our own government. It was an unfortunate situation for all concerned. I also reported to my management what had happened the night before. I showed them Jim's business card and explained his problem and the serious threat to his livelihood. I told them how I tried to calm down this furious individual, listening to his complaints before I could get a word in edgewise. Bill began calling me "Cool Hand Luci." I was proud of that nickname because it was, to me, more than just a term of endearment. It meant that I had stood up under a very real test, had kept calm and cool in a furnace situation, and had come through it in some measure of growth. There's a Bible verse in Hebrews 12 which says:

Being punished isn't enjoyable while it is happening—it hurts! But afterwards we can see the result, a quiet growth in grace and character.

Our work can be very difficult at times. But those long, hard, seemingly endless days, months, and years that we pour into the jobs or careers we have chosen are designed by God to build a team spirit, to forge out a personal sense of growth when we "go it alone," and to encourage us to overleap obstacles which may arise in our pathways.

Sir William Osler, the famed physician and professor of medicine, once said of work:

> It is the open sesame to every portal, the great equalizer in the world, the true philosopher's stone which transmutes all the base metal of humanity into gold.

After twenty-five years with Mobil, I can vouch for that, because I am a product of that alchemy. And I'm so glad.

SOLITUDE

I have a passionate love for solitude and silence.
I can gaze for hours at a fire or the sea without
feeling any need for additional companionship.

I took this little poll once. I asked ten people the same question: "If you had ten dollars in your pocket and you were commanded to spend it on something absolutely impractical, what would you buy?"

Oh brother! You should have heard the variety of answers on that one. A couple of people, rather structured in their thinking and planning, didn't know how they'd spend it. Couldn't decide. They debated and debated in their minds, but there were just too many options. They never came up with an answer. Another guy said, "Well, I'd buy and eat Haagen Daz ice cream until I got sick and died."

"I'd buy that record I've been wanting," somebody else said . . . or "I'd take my buddy out for a large pizza, but he'd have to add money to it 'cause ten bucks won't buy a large pizza any more." And don't you like this response? "I'd make a down payment on silk sheets."

All sorts of answers. Try asking it sometime and see what you get. Know what I'd buy? I'd go down to the local flower shop and blow the whole ten dollars on daffodils. Nothing else. Just daffodils. Then I'd come home, divide them up, and put them in vases in every room in the house.

I *love* daffodils. They are my favorite flower. Simple, sprightly, and silent, they keep me company in quiet moments of contemplation. William Wordsworth expressed it much better than I in the closing verse of his well-known poem about daffodils:

> For oft, when on my couch I lie
> In vacant or in pensive mood,
> They flash upon that inward eye
> Which is the bliss of solitude;
> And then my heart with pleasure fills,
> And dances with the daffodils.[1]

Perhaps I find them good company because I am often "in vacant or in pensive mood." It is certainly true that the older I get, the more reflective and contemplative I become. During my father's last years upon the earth I used to see such a faraway look in his eyes, and occasionally I'd say, "What are you thinking, Daddy? You look so pensive."

"Oh," he'd answer, rather apologetically, "I guess I was just letting my mind float back to the past. I was reflecting upon bygone days. Can't even tell you exactly what I was thinking, but it was nice. Maybe I was actually *not* thinking."

Not thinking! I like that . . . and I do it, too. I let my mind drift around and stop where it wants, without command or duties. I let it run its own course and take me with it wherever it wants to go. I allow "the bliss of solitude" to be in charge, and off I go to the private delights of my heart. A great part of solitude was made for dreaming, gazing, drifting, floating—anything but conscious thinking. It was designed for the soft company of a crackling fire, a rippling brook, a Mozart melody, a snowfall, a soaring bird, a gentle rain, falling leaves, or dancing daffodils. At those moments, I don't have to think; I just have to be and it's enough.

Sometimes my life cannot bear one more requirement. My mind can't assimilate another fact. That's when the wholesome, high enjoyment of solitude reaches its most alluring proportions. It seems I cannot get to that blissful state fast enough,

---

1. William Wordsworth, *Poems, Lyrics, Sonnets* (Mount Vernon: The Peter Pauper Press, no date), p. 56.

simply to come away before I come apart. Every human being has that need, I believe; the need to float with voluntary inertia, in limbo, which frees us (at least momentarily) from the burdens and stresses of life. I had an instructor in a management seminar recently who said, "We must all learn how to steal and lie— how to steal away and lie down." A clever way to word a universal demand.

It is in those moments of solitude that I find unsolicited refreshment. There in the quietness, I often give birth to my best and most creative ideas. If I am tired, I find rest. If I'm disorganized, I discover and collect loose ends. If I'm fed up with the daily grind of deadlines and activity, that tranquility provides the peace I need to work through irritability or fretfulness. During those moments or hours of solitude, which are vital to my soul, the better part of me emerges. Again, as our friend Wordsworth said, when I'm "sick of business and tired of pleasures, how gracious, how benign is solitude." As the first daffodils of spring are to a war-torn battlefield, so is solitude to the conflicts in my troubled heart.

It would appear I've been that way since I was a child. At the age of three or four (from my mother's records), I learned and began singing my first song, "Lazy Bones." Only, being unable to pronounce my *l*'s, I sang "Wazy Bones."

Wazy Bones, sweepin' in the sun,
Sweepin' in the mornin'
'Til the noon work's done.
Sweepin' in the mornin' sun,
Sweepin' 'til the noon work's done.

Ambitious child! Upon hearing that, my parents probably wondered what kind of future lay ahead for their offspring when one of her first utterances to the world spoke of laziness . . . or rather, "waziness." But I suppose even then, long before I became cognizant of the fact that life was going to be filled with stress and turmoil, I was unconsciously, but prophetically, preparing myself for the rest and the calmness that I would one day carve out in order to cope. At least I interpret it that way, knowing my temperament now.

Since those early days of toddling around, chanting that little ditty, I have always cherished special, private times for myself. Times of doing nothing. But I have a different name for it now, although it's not a bit more sophisticated. Instead of "sweepin' in the sun," I call it "putzing about." It is a completely satisfying experience with powers of rejuvenation . . . in my "vacant or pensive" moods. As my brother, Chuck, agrees from his writing:

> That doesn't mean a lazy, irresponsible lifestyle full of indolence and free from industry. No, this is first and foremost a *mental* rest . . . a refusal to churn, to fret, to strive.[2]

If somebody asked what I do when I putz about, I might be hard pressed to answer. I'd have to say, "Well, different things: I water plants. I look at the sky. I reflect on the past. I laugh at an idea. I rearrange a bookshelf. I walk on the beach. I sing. I count stars. I look through my photo albums. I read old letters. I fly a kite. I stare into space. I do what I feel like doing and be what I feel like being. But it is *always* simple, uninvolved, and alone." Solitude, in this way, provides the space my body needs to relax and regroup. And I have never yet found an adequate substitute for what putzing about does for me.

The second noteworthy benefit from time alone is that it provides a climate for my mind to cultivate and produce. Even though this is in direct antithesis to the idea of bodily relaxation, it has equal value. For me to read, I must have quietude. When I listen to a symphony with a view toward understanding what I'm hearing, I prefer to be alone; otherwise it becomes "background music." And, most especially, when I write—letters, articles, or a book—I cannot deal with outside distractions. I become extremely one-tracked, undivided in my attention.

---

2. Charles R. Swindoll, *Growing Strong in the Seasons of Life* (Portland, Oreg.: Multnomah Press, 1983), p. 210.

This demands absolute solitude, a sort of "self-imposed solitary confinement," if you will.

Let me say here, as an aside, that writing is a fickle partner. You can never predict when it will cooperate. As someone has aptly put it: "Writing is easy; all you do is sit staring at a blank sheet of paper until the drops of blood form on your forehead." I have planned entire weekends around the task of composing a chapter and nothing will come together. My creative juices seem to be either dried up or frozen. Then at 2:30 A.M. of the following Monday, I awaken with a "brilliant" idea and cannot seem to write down my thoughts rapidly enough. They tumble out, one over the other. If I knew how or why that happens, believe me, I'd set about to correct it. But . . . who can predict the time, date, and place of the writer's ideas? Thoreau kept a piece of paper under his pillow, and when he could not sleep or was awakened with an idea, he wrote in the dark. I've done that. However, there's a problem the next morning of trying to decipher and interpret one's nocturnal hieroglyphics! But one thing is certain for me, my best writing efforts come in solitude.

I was amused about two weeks ago in connection with this very issue. I had bought a recording of sonatas for piano and wind instruments by the twentieth century French composer, Francis Poulenc, and on the back of the album cover, there were a few comments made by Poulenc in an interview. He was describing his methods of musical composition:

> I compose as seems best to me when the wish takes me. I envy composers like Milhaud and Hindemith who can write wherever they happen to be. I'm extremely susceptible visually, everything is an excuse for getting sidetracked, for frittering away my time. So, I have to retire within myself and work in solitude.

I can identify wholeheartedly. If there is anything to distract me, it will: noise, music, children, television, friends, the telephone. I have to purposely cultivate an environment which will offer the least distraction away from everyone and everything. I have to rid myself of all my "natural enemies." Poulenc went on:

> Contrary to what is generally believed, I don't work easily. My first drafts, written in a sort of strange musical shorthand, are full of crossings-out.[3]

Again, so familiar. This entire book has been written in longhand with deletions. Additions. Crossings-out. Tearings-up. Startings over. Are there such words? Maybe not, but there are such actions, because I've done them—over and over. I've mumbled in my moments of discouragement, "Isn't there a short cut in all this? I'm *never* going to get through." But there isn't. The only way to do it is to do it. Bit by bit. Page by page. As slow going as it seems, that's the only way I can write. It is "my method," and my thoughts don't disentangle themselves until I sit over a pad of paper, pen in hand, and start in. As Jimmy Durante wisely said, "Dese are de conditions dat prevail." Everybody has his or her creative style, and when that style is not followed, creativity is thwarted.

My companions for writing are solitude and silence. They establish the climate for my mind to plant seeds, cultivate thoughts, and bear fruit.

Third, and perhaps the most blissful aspect of solitude, is that it provides the leisure needed for my spirit to discern and decide. It gives me an opportunity to get apart from other duties and communicate with God. A few days ago I had a blessed (and interesting!) experience in prayer during an hour of solitude. Actually, I was on the Los Angeles freeway, which is always a good time to pray for at least two obvious reasons: I take my life in my hands while there, and since I am an hour from work by the freeway system, there's much time to pray. I was on my way to work on a Monday morning.

First of all, I told the Lord that I would like him to be my counselor for that hour, and as is true of all qualified counselors, he'd listen and I'd talk. Then, when I had finished, I would appreciate his clarifying my problems for me, giving me discernment on how to handle them and showing me a new direction

---

3. Francis Poulenc, *Poulenc* (New York: Nonesuch Records, 1983), back cover.

through them. I talked out loud as though we were the only two on that frantic freeway. Well, we were—at least in *my* car. Hey, maybe my next book could be *Prayer Life in the Fast Lane.*

I started off by saying,

> Lord, this morning I'm thinking about a verse in Proverbs 20: "Counsel in the heart of a man is like deep water; but a man of understanding will draw it out." You know the verse, Lord. For some reason that sticks in my mind today. I want so much for you to be that "man of understanding" and draw out the counsel I need from the deep water of my heart, as I tell you about a problem I have. Help me to be totally honest.

Then I told the Lord about the heartache I was experiencing in a relationship with a friend, someone I had loved for years but with whom I felt *I* was doing all the giving. I expressed how much I resented this friend's inconsistency in the relationship—an "on again, off again" thing. The only thing that seemed to be consistent was the inconsistency. I told him that even though I loved the individual and wanted to be tenacious and faithful, I was discouraged and I felt maybe I should quit trying. What did he think?

During my prayer I cited examples of how the lack of consistency actually manifested itself in the relationship (exactly as though I were talking with a counselor). Occasionally there would be extended pauses as I drove along. I tried to assess where my spirit was at each moment, wanting to be sensitive to the voice of God if he wished to say something to me. This was not the only issue I prayed about, but I would say it was my primary prayer topic. I knew very well that God was hearing me. I perceived it in my spirit, and as my stream of consciousness emerged in audible prayer, my burdens seemed to lift. By relating my troubled heart to him, I was being released from the weight of it, somehow.

I prayed for about forty minutes, and just as I turned off the freeway onto a surface street, it was as though I heard a little voice say, "You're not always so consistent in *our* relationship

155

either, Luci."What? I listened more intently, more within myself now, because I knew I was beginning to hear counsel from the "deep water" of my own heart, just as Proverbs had stated. The voice continued, "Haven't there been times when I've done all the loving and the giving and you've been 'off again, on again' with me, too? Give your friend a break. Try not to judge. Don't hold a resentment. Just trust me and wait. And keep remembering— you're not always as consistent as you pride yourself in being— at least with me, you're not, and I'm God."

Wow! I'm here to tell you, friends, that was a very real time of discernment in prayer. In my communication with the Lord, I received clarity in a problem I had, not to mention conviction!

I expressed my heart to the Lord, thanking him for showing me I was no different from the person I was complaining about— that my pride had not let me see my own error in it all. And you know why? Because I hadn't gotten quiet long enough. All I had done, up to that moment, was complain. But in the car, alone with him in our place of solitude, we met and he provided the tranquility and direction I needed. The problem itself wasn't eliminated. It didn't magically vanish, but the revelation of a judgmental attitude in me toward my friend became clear when I realized I was just as inconsistent in my relationship with God, who mattered a great deal more than that friend. I could look at the problem from a brand new perspective, and that helped me a lot in getting a handle on how to pray about it in the future.

I was about two miles from work and decided to close my "quiet time" (I hate that overused term!) with music on the radio. When I flipped it on, guess what was playing? A poignant song that I love in all its sadness, from the Alan Parsons Project, en- titled "Silence and I":

> If I cried out loud over sorrows I've known
>   And the secrets I've heard
> It would ease my mind, someone sharing the load
>   But I won't breathe a word
> We're two of a kind, silence and I.
> We need a chance to talk things over
> Two of a kind, silence and I.

We'll find a way to work it out.

While the children laughed, I was always afraid
    Of the smile of the clown
So I close my eyes till I can't see the light
    And I hide from the sun.
We're two of a kind, silence and I,
We need a chance to talk things over.
Two of a kind, silence and I.
We'll find a way to work it out.

I can hear the cry of the leaf on a tree
    As it falls to the ground.
I can hear the call of an echoing voice
    And there's no one around.
We're two of a kind, silence and I
We need a chance to talk things over.
Two of a kind, silence and I.
We'll find a way to work it out.[4]

Please know that I am not dumb, young, or naive enough to believe that solitude will always be without loneliness. I have experienced loneliness in those moments of "silence and I." I know what it is to feel bereft of friends, companionship, and affection. Like Alan Parsons, I've "cried out loud from the sorrows I've known." I've heard "the call of an echoing voice, and there's no one around." It's tough. It's sad. And it's lonely. Every human being has felt those feelings in times of solitude.

I know too that there is a very real possibility, as I grow older, that the loneliness which often accompanies solitude will fall my lot to a greater degree than ever before. Friends of mine will pass away. I may have to consider uncertain health. I must endure the renunciation of various activities. We all know that aging brings infirmities and at its end stands death. This is reality, and to deny it would be sticking my head in the sand. But I refuse to live there.

Solitude is a blessing, not a curse. It provides the space for

my body to relax and regroup. The climate for my mind to cultivate and produce. The leisure for my spirit to discern and decide.
And what I glean from all that *now*, I trust will be the food on
which I am nourished *then*, in years to come. It will be my gift to
myself for old age. Ah! Then truly my heart will with pleasure fill,
and dance with the daffodils.

CHURCH

God does not have a name . . . He is too big to fit inside names. A name is a prison, God is free.

I live one block from a church, a Presbyterian church. At this very moment, while I am writing, it is six o'clock in the evening, and each day at this hour, to designate the time, the church bell rings and hymns are played whose melodies waft throughout the neighborhood. It's a lovely sound which I enjoy daily. Not only is it beautiful, but it forces me to stop whatever I'm doing and think about those hymns. Presently, the melody that's ringing through the air is "O Zion, Haste," the fourth verse of which I have loved for years and memorized after I found it typed out and taped in the front of my mother's Bible:

> Give of thy sons to bear the message glorious;
> Give of thy wealth to speed them on their way;
> Pour out thy soul for them in prayer victorious;
> And all thou spendest, Jesus will repay.
> Publish glad tidings, tidings of peace;
> Tidings of Jesus, redemption and release.

From my earliest recollections of life, church—the local church that is—was an integral part of my rearing. We as a family were involved in practically every conceivable facet of the organized church: membership and attendance, the sacraments, worship services, church foundings, church splits, church "hopping," the teaching ministry, choir, boards, vacation Bible school committees, Sunday school classes, Bible classes, and church camps. If my memory serves me correctly, there has also been at least one occasion per sibling when either my brothers or myself was left at the church, accidentally forgotten.

Hearing those church bells, in fact, reminds me of the time a friend of mine and I, as teenagers, crawled into the baptistry of our church and stayed there, lying on the bottom of it throughout the evening service while trying to control our giggling. We did remarkably well until the very last amen after the benediction, when the church bells were rung, much to our surprise. At first we were scared half to death; then we looked at each other and exploded into laughter. I'm not sure anyone in the congregation heard us amidst the ringing of the bells. We were so busy crawling out of there, we never stopped to ask.

When I consider church in my life, it brings to mind bittersweet thoughts. There is much about church that I love and from which I have benefited and do benefit greatly. The majority of my most valuable biblical foundations have come through a church Bible class, teachings of doctrines and their value in application to my experience. Since I love music and enjoy singing, sacred music has had a significant place in my life—the singing and memorizing of hymns as well as participation in choir and ensemble work. Then, of course, corporate worship among a body of people who embrace the same theology as I has provided many happy hours of praising God. All of this has aided me in forming my outlook on life in general and the foundation of the ongoing building of my character in particular. But there is also a part of church which I find to be poignantly sad, a basic inherent deficiency which I have observed again and again throughout my life in churches of different denominations and locations.

Looking at the total aspect of church, then, from a bittersweet point of view, let me approach the subject using that as a springboard for my thoughts. First the sweet, since it is my idealistic nature to see the best at the outset.

A number of years ago I became actively involved with a Bible class in a sizable church in Houston, Texas. When I say "actively," I mean that in capital letters and neon lights. I attended class four nights a week for over a year, made notebooks, took copious notes in my Bible, and underlined everything I thought was important. All of my friends at the time, along with various members of my family, were doing the same. We were gung ho in every sense of the word. We talked, ate, met, slept the Bible. It was as though, for me personally, I had arrived at a banquet table of delicious, abundant courses of food after literally years of reluctantly eating only enough average fare to keep me alive. I will never forget those classes nor the feelings of nourishment and subsequent satisfaction I was experiencing, really for the first time. I felt full. And when we're full, we're happy—so I felt happy as well.

Better still, what I was learning, when applied to my daily life, was working. As I said earlier, I was eagerly trying to apply doctrine to experience, and everything about my "insides" felt reborn: my walk with God, my prayer life, my attitudes toward problem areas, dealing with guilt, coming to know and understand myself. Not only did I feel wonderful but I was acquiring knowledge to support my feelings. And in problem areas, where I was without clarity, I somehow knew that in time I would acquire insight into those problems, or I would realize the lack of clarity was a universal quandary, not something that was a flaw only found in my makeup. To put it simply, I felt my life was going in the right direction. As the Holy Spirit began to illumine my pathway, I began walking in light, and the more I stepped out in faith, the more light I was given. Let me make an understatement: It was glorious!

Coupled with this almost indulgent exposure to the teachings of the Bible, I began an indepth study of a doctrine that I had never before understood or lived by although it could have been mine for the taking from the moment of my salvation years before—the doctrine of grace. Grace, in all its richness and liberty, was made clear to me; that is, as clearly as the human mind can understand it. With my discovery of this new doctrine, there also came the unraveling of a number of puzzles I had battled for years.

1. Since God was completely satisfied with Christ's death on the cross, God was not interested in my attempt to make points with him or to perform in some manner in order to be acceptable to him. All I had to do for acceptability was believe what Christ had done in my behalf. Therefore I could relax, quit performing, and be completely myself.

2. Grace gave me a "position" in Christ at the moment of my belief, and it perfected me for the future I would spend in heaven. Therefore I could quit trying to be a perfectionist myself, because I was now already perfect "by position" in Christ.

3. Since Christ was the complete fulfillment of the law, I, as a Christian, no longer believed that salvation from God came by keeping the law. Through the Spirit of God, any one of the Ten Commandments could be produced in my life. Therefore they, in and of themselves, ceased to be my standard for living. My new commandment for living was the grace of God and the liberty I had found in Christ.

4. If I slipped into an activity that I realized was wrong or sinful, my way back to God didn't come through some harsh penance or self-inflicted guilt. I simply had to confess what I had done before God and name it for what it was. Therefore my fears of doing the wrong things and subsequent punishment by God were nullified, or at least minimized. I enjoyed sweeter fellowship with God and found myself more desirous of pleasing him.

5. With the coming of grace into my life, I now realized Christ and the Holy Spirit actually lived in me. Therefore my decisions and attitudes could be the result of a "faith-rest" theology rather than a "work-do" theology.

These new concepts became mine, plus many, many more. As you read this you may think, "That's basic information, Luci . . . all Christians are taught that." And while I would like to agree with you, I cannot. I know for a fact that there are many well-meaning, law-abiding, church-going Christians out there who are starving to death, because I used to be one of them. It's tragic, but it's true.

Some time after I began to apply the doctrine of grace to my daily experience, I discovered a wonderful book entitled *Dispensationalism Today,* by Charles Ryrie. My logical mind latched onto it immediately, and I devoured its contents. In fact, I've re-read it on two or three different occasions. The thrilling thing about Dr. Ryrie's teaching is that it makes such good sense, as well as the fact that it gives grace its proper place of pre-eminence in the dispensation in which we live—the Church Age, or the Dispensation of Grace. Although this might not be a point of view you embrace, I would have to say it has opened a whole new world of spiritual insight for me. Ryrie says:

> To be sure the dispensationalist does not say that there was no grace ever displayed before the coming of Christ (any more than he says there is no law after His coming), but the Scriptures do say that His coming displayed the grace of God in such brightness that all previous displays could be considered as nothing. Under grace the responsibility on man is to accept the gift of righteousness which God freely offers to all (Romans 5:15-18). There are two aspects of the grace of God in this economy: (1) the blessing is entirely of grace, and (2) that grace is for all.[1]

And I love this:

> Dispensation does foster Bible study, and if with that comes a dissatisfaction with an existing fellowship, it is not surprising. If Reformers feel that they can best serve the Lord outside the Roman church, or Scots outside the Church of Scotland, or Baptists outside the state church, or dispensationalists outside a denomination, is this necessarily wrong?[2]

1. Charles C. Ryrie, *Dispensationalism Today* (Chicago: Moody Press, 1965), pp. 62-63.

2. Ryrie, *Dispensationalism,* p. 83.

Ryrie's book only reiterates the freedom and liberty I have found in Christ. It helps me to understand that supernatural living is opened up to me because of this personal, loving, intimate unity I now enjoy with Christ. The freedom Christ offers does not give me permission to do as I please. On the contrary, it provides the avenue to believe God, obey him, take him at his word, and then watch him work in my life since I am no longer in charge or bound hand and foot by the dos and don'ts of the Law. Grace means looking at life in all its positiveness rather than living by a standard of negatives. Grace, to me, frees the heart of an individual to carve out a singular, creative relationship with God through Jesus Christ. There are no formalities or requirements for performance.

This brings me to the bitter part of my bittersweet thoughts about the church. Unfortunately, wherever there is liberty in Christ or the operation of a Spirit-filled life as opposed to a life lived under the law, there is always somebody ready to pounce on that freedom. I have heard it said that one of the most unbecoming things about Christianity is Christians themselves, and I have found that to be true many times. I've witnessed in others and experienced for myself judgment, intolerance, even rejection by fellow Christians, simply because there was not an acceptable level of performance or conformity on the part of the person being judged. The very thing that the church professes to have, namely love and acceptance, is often the thing that is flagrantly lacking among its own members. Why? Why do we Christians think that we have the right to tell people how to live before God? How do we have the effrontery to do God's job? It is certainly our responsibility to present the gospel to the unbelieving world, and being caretakers of the truth of scripture we are equally responsible to encourage and disciple fellow Christians in their walk of faith, lovingly admonishing those who are going headlong down a wayward path. But we are never given the right to judge or condemn others. That is the exclusive responsibility of God's Holy Spirit and the Bible.

Francis Schaeffer captures my thought in this excerpt from his book, *The Church at the End of the Twentieth Century:*

The observable and practical love in our day should also without reservation cut across all such lines as language, nationalities, national frontiers, younger or older, colors of skin, education and economic levels, accent, line of birth, the class system of our particular locality, dress, short and long hair among whites and African and non-African hairdos among blacks, the wearing of shoes and the non-wearing of shoes, cultural differentiations, and the more traditional and less traditional forms of worship.[3]

Let somebody in the local church show a crack in his or her life and what happens? Fellow church members are all over him, trying to straighten him out. Whatever it is that's on our "rejection list," we camp on that, outlining ways for certain people to behave so they will be acceptable to God. But what we are *really* saying is "so they will be acceptable to us." Mind you, I am not condoning sin, and I believe the Bible makes it clear what sin is, but here's what I find deeply regrettable: The Bible stands in judgment of sin—and it has the right to do so—but the church stands in judgment of the sinner—and has no right to do so. We *are* the church. We *are* the sinners, and repentance will not come when we do the judging of each other. Admonition and judgment are two different things, and nowhere do these concepts need to be more clearly defined and carried out than in the church. I have found (as in the classic example of my father's treatment of me so many years ago when I was a legalistic brat) that only tolerance and acceptance lead to repentance.

The twentieth century church has a way of throwing out the baby with the bath water, and I believe that is a shame when we, of all people in time, have access to God's greatest declaration and abundance of grace. Not only do we need that grace in dealing with the shortcomings and disappointments in ourselves, but we need it in dealing with other people and their faults.

3. Francis A. Schaeffer, *The Church at the End of the Twentieth Century* (Downers Grove, Ill.: Inter-Varsity Press, 1971), p. 106.

Let me recall two examples (completely unrelated) which capture the essence of what I'm trying to say. Each example has to do with Christian friends of mine, both church members, living in other states. The first experience is centered around a friend I'll call Jane, who decided to separate from her husband while she attempted to work through a number of inequities in her marriage. Not only was she trying to come to grips with her own thoughts, but she was trying to sort through her emotions as well—guilt, fear, submission, rejection—all those common feelings we all face when working through problems.

During this period of time, Jane desperately needed a support system, so she naturally turned to her closest friends—a small group of women in her church who were also married and with whom she had shared her deepest joys and sorrows up to that time. Women she and her husband knew well. She needed their sanctuary and their understanding and she turned to them to bounce her thoughts and feelings off of.

When Jane told of her decision to separate from her husband, she received instead of understanding and sanctuary a cold, calculated, and very real attack against her decision and her person. In fact, Jane's friends refused to *speak* to her until there was a workable reconciliation with her husband. There arose a severe estrangement between the friends and Jane. This action on the part of her "support team" hurt her deeply. Nevertheless, she continued to try to clear the air between them, but to no avail. Later she moved away. She wrote her friends in an effort to regain their lost love and support. No response. They never provided the tolerance and acceptance that Jane wanted—and needed.

Finally Jane divorced her husband, and that really set the wheels of accusation in motion. Not only did Jane's friends write scathing letters of judgment to her, but they reported all they knew to their minister, who took their side and joined them in their debate: church friends vs. Jane! As long as five years after the divorce, Jane's former minister was seeking to bring Jane to a position of conformity, and the only words he had for her when they occasionally met were words of judgment and correction.

Now I ask you, where is the love in all of this? Where is the sanctuary of friendship among church friends who allegedly believe as we do? Jane had a very active conscience and the Holy Spirit was doing his own convicting in certain areas in her heart. She didn't need five years of negative, condemning reminders from erstwhile friends and a former minister.

The second illustration is vastly different from the first, and it brings to my mind one of the saddest memories of my life. A tragedy in every sense of the word.

Many years ago I was involved in a series of voice lessons which I took from a personal friend, a vocal coach by profession who lived in a nearby town. I'll refer to him as Bob. Bob was a Christian, a graduate of a well-known Christian university in the field of music, with a beautiful voice. I knew him to be a sensitive person with a warm personality and a great sense of humor. Not only did we get together to work on my voice—I'd sing and he'd coach me—but a few times we had lunch together, and often we'd linger over our coffee cups, talking for hours, cracking jokes or discussing deep issues of our souls—theology, music, books. It was wonderful fun and we both enjoyed it and benefited from it.

Bob was in his thirties, unmarried, living alone, and a time or two during one of our marathon conversations he would confide in me his personal battles with homosexuality. He exhibited great concern that he seemed unable to overcome certain behavior patterns he had observed in himself. He didn't want these patterns to become a life style because of his Christian convictions.

Bob attended a local church in his neighborhood where he was actively involved in the music program, and he told me he had a number of friends in that church with whom he often spent evenings having dinner and engaging in what he called "surface table conversation." They were his Christian support system, in a sense. One night when Bob was unusually troubled in his spirit over his guilt feelings regarding homosexuality, he opened his heart to these Christian friends. He confessed his feelings and his fears. He told them of some of the battles he was having in his troubled soul.

Do you know his friends' response? They condemned him. They told him they questioned his commitment to Christ if he had those kinds of feelings. They quoted scripture to him. They never understood that he was seeking their love and understanding, not their correction. And . . . as if their reaction were not judgmental enough, they reported his confession to the senior pastor of their church so that Bob could be publicly reprimanded, and set about "cleaning up his life and thoughts." Two or three days later, on a Tuesday evening, Bob phoned me and told me what had occurred with those church members. Now added to his deep fears regarding his sexual orientation there was the very real and new fear of public exposure. He said he felt like he was drowning. He was heartbroken, and between sobs on the phone he told me of his tremendous regret in being so transparent with "those so-called Christians." He also said that he felt sure he was going to be condemned before an entire congregation the following Sunday.

I was stunned! I could hardly believe what he was reporting. It just didn't make sense. I cried with Bob on the phone and I tried to assure him that a public reprimand would never take place. That was barbaric. His minister had to be more understanding than those other people. I tried everything I could think of to encourage Bob to hang on, but apparently it all fell on deaf ears.

The following Friday night, about 8 o'clock, there was a knock at my front door. When I opened it, there stood a man whom I did not know well but whom I had met through Bob. He too was a musician. His face was full of anguish and I could see the evidence of nervousness written all over him. I invited him in. As he was coming through the door, he said, "Luci, Bob is dead." Silence—

Then he stopped, looked straight at me, and quietly continued speaking. "Earlier this evening he lay down on his bed, put a gun to his mouth, and blew his head off."

I thought I would collapse. A million clanging bells rang in my head. My brain kept repeating ". . . blew his head off . . . blew his head off." I simply couldn't believe it. "I just talked with him this week!" Then I vividly recalled his fears, the anguish in his voice, the regret he felt over being transparent with "those so-called Christians." And I wept.

Later I attended Bob's funeral. A cold, unfeeling, plastic ceremony of putting the dead to rest. So without warmth and heart. But here's the thing that has stuck with me all these years: Seated a few feet away from me in that funeral service was Bob's mother. Dressed in black and broken in spirit, she was completely grief-stricken. As the service was conducted and as we sat not more than five feet apart, I occasionally heard her almost inaudible whisper, "Why?" The tormented cry of a heart that was left to wonder about the untimely and unexplainable death of her son. As I sat there, her whispered *why* was like the shot heard 'round the world.

Why did that tragedy have to happen? What could any of us have done to prevent it? How did the seedbed for such an outcome first occur? These are questions that cannot be answered with accuracy because every answer opens the door to another question. But I do know this: Our lack of judgment over another's area of sin or weakness carries a far greater possibility toward repentance than does a spirit of correction or condemnation. In the case of Jane or in the tragedy of Bob, that same principle applies.

At this juncture, let me make myself perfectly clear. In these two illustrations, the issue is not divorce or homosexuality. The issue is one Christian's treatment of another. When people are hurting and need our support, let's give it with a whole and understanding heart. And when admonition is required, let's give it with careful and loving sensitivity. And when judgment is the answer, let's leave that up to God.

No one has the absolute worst problems in the world and no one has the absolute best advice to give. We're all in this struggle together. We are all students of Life. Read this, if you will, from a man who was born a Negro slave in the middle of the 1800s:

> How far you go in life depends on your being tender
> with the young, compassionate with the aged,

sympathetic with the striving and tolerant of the weak and the strong. Because someday in life you will have been all of these.

George Washington Carver

Sometimes we're up, at other times we're down, but we need each other. We need others to let us be ourselves—especially those of like faith, on whom we can depend and to whom we should be able to turn for solace. By the same token, we need to allow others to be themselves. Maybe what I'm looking for among a body of Christians doesn't exist. Maybe I'm hoping for too much. What my spirit reaches out for is that group of people who accept me as I am—warts and all! I'm looking for that support team. I'm looking for that kind of encouragement. I'm looking for a church body that won't always knock me dead with scripture or spiritualize everything in life. And tell me, aren't you looking for the same thing?

If the church has taught me anything, it has—in a strange, unintentional, backhanded sort of way—taught me to value my freedom. Freedom is the natural (and supernatural) by-product of God's grace. It is the gift of God for me to be myself. Through some bitter lessons I have learned that no church member, no fellow Christian has the right to press me into his or her performance mold. More important, I won't let them do it to me any more, nor do I want to do it to them. When I latched onto a knowledge of grace, I also latched onto the liberty that comes with it. I learned how to live abundantly, and that, once and for all, has killed the desire to go back to a narrow, miserly, predictable existence. I'm free now, and I love it. Like Kazantzakis. Ryrie. Schaeffer. Carver. I'm free from bondage. Free from the law. Free from prejudicial living. Free from wanting to judge others. I've learned the truth, and it has set me free. Remember what the apostle Paul said in a letter he once wrote to a church?

> So Christ has made us free. Now make sure that you stay free and don't get all tied up again in the chains of slavery.

TRAVELS

I was roaming in order to become acquainted with Attica, or so I thought. But I was really roaming in order to become acquainted with my soul.

W hat a liftoff! Other than an occasional "whoosh" from the heater, I heard no sound. Yet there we were, floating in a basket above the earth, heading toward heaven. It was early in the morning on a nippy spring day and it was our first (and only) time to go hot air ballooning. I had been given the trip as a Christmas gift from Kurt, my generous, adventuresome friend, but it never materialized due to bad weather. So here, five months later, we were "cashing in on the goods." We ballooned (or would you say "floated"?) for an hour, then returned to earth to talk about it the rest of our lives. If you have never been, you should go. It's great, and it will definitely give you the lift you need.

Traveling, in almost any form, on almost every conveyance conceivable, is one of my greatest joys. You name it—boat, car, plane, train, van, motorcycle, donkey, truck, bike, horse, or hot air balloon—I'm on it. I'm outa' here! I *love* to travel. I love the squiggles I get while I'm packing; I love the excitement I feel at the moment of departure, and I love the adventure of being gone and having a new experience. Don't you think almost everyone feels that way? I know of very few people who don't get excited over the prospect of a trip, even if it's only for a weekend or overnight.

About three years ago I read *Travels with Charley*, by John Steinbeck, a delightful and sympathetic book filled with his observations about America and Americans. Charley, Steinbeck's French poodle, and John made this trip together in 1960 when the author was almost sixty years old. They traveled the length and breadth of the United States in a three-quarter-ton pickup truck that Steinbeck named Rocinante (the name of Don Quixote's horse). After the journey was over, he put many of his observations about life in the book. Wonderful, revealing scraps of conversation, indepth thoughts on loneliness, and his illuminating, panoramic view of our land and its people.

In fact, it's an ironic thing, but I read the book while I too was traveling. I remember lying on the beach of the Greek island of Poros, reading at leisure and laughing at Steinbeck's colorful and salty humor. It often interrupted the sleep of Sophia, lying beside me, and I'd say to her, "Hey, you've got to hear this. It's hilarious, and so true of Americans . . ." Then I'd read an excerpt to my captive audience of one. Scribbled in the back of my weatherbeaten paperback copy of *Travels with Charley* are these words: "Completed 6-21-80, in flight from Rome to Boston." (I am so glad I have have the inadvertent good sense to write down tidbits of information like that through the years. Otherwise I never could have remembered all this stuff. And . . . I certainly couldn't have written the many details to which I have made reference in the volume you are now holding.)

Anyway . . . back to the subject at hand. Near the beginning of the book, Steinbeck makes a striking observation that I think is worth noting here, because I find it to be a universal characteristic, not only in America, but everywhere I have traveled. He's talking about his neighbors who came to say good-bye before he and Charley departed:

> I saw in their eyes something I was to see over and over in every part of the nation—a burning desire to go, to move, to get underway, anyplace, away from any Here. They spoke quietly of how they wanted to go someday, to move about, free and unanchored, not toward something but away from something. I saw this look

and heard this yearning everywhere, in every state I visited.[1]

While I was on that Greek island for a week with my friend, Sophia, each day we went to the beach, swam in the sea, and sunbathed on the rocks. One morning as we were approaching "our" rocks, we saw a young man already there. He had laid his backpack on the stone next to where he was sitting, and he was staring out into the Aegean with a placid look on his face . . . daydreaming, no doubt, of the never-never land he hoped to reach at his journey's end.

We walked up to him, introduced ourselves, and saw that he was an American. After a few pleasantries and small talk, Sophia left to go swimming and I continued conversation with the young traveler. He was tall, very polite, and quite handsome, tanned from the Greek sun. He had been backpacking alone across Europe and Greece and was now about eight weeks into his excursion, which was going to last ten weeks. He told me he was a college student ("a senior, finally") from a well-known American university and an architecture major. He had saved his money in order to take this trip—his lifelong dream.

I asked him how he liked Greece, and of course he said all the usual things people say when they travel in Greece—"Oh, it's beautiful. The people are friendly; the villages are picturesque and unspoiled . . . and the islands are like jewels sparkling in the ocean. I love it." Then he said the most interesting thing which caught and held me in rapt attention. My eyes were riveted to his face, which certainly wasn't a difficult exercise with his looks! He spoke with sincere expression and eagerness, almost as if he had been waiting for me to arrive in order to tell me this . . . and maybe he had.

"You know," he said, "when I left America, two months ago, I was dying to get away from there. I somehow had

---

1. John Steinbeck, *Travels with Charley* (New York: Bantam Books, 1966), p. 10.

this burning desire to go . . . just go. I don't know why, really, except inside of me I knew I had to get underway. I felt I was running away from something, and at the same time, running toward something. Yet the harder I've run and the further I've come, the more this 'thing' in me is in hot pursuit, and the more distant is the 'something' I'm running toward. You know what I mean?"

"Yes, I think I do," I said, feeling such strange affinity with this unknown person who was expressing some of the same thoughts I, too, had had many years before, and who sounded like he was quoting right out of the paperback I was holding in my hand. It was eerie—a bit like I was talking with a reincarnated John Steinbeck or something. "Go on . . ."

"Well," he continued, "the strangest thing is that now I wonder if that 'thing' from which I am running is trying to give me some kind of message."

"Really? Like what?" I asked.

"Like, why are you running from me? I *am* you! What you're looking for in leaving America is inside of you. You're searching for me . . . your soul, and I'm in here, waiting for you to find me."

Needless to say, I was utterly fascinated! This was *my* kind of conversation. I wanted to respond with, "Will you marry me?" but realizing that 1) I was probably twice his age, and 2) marrying me would *really* foul up his pilgrimage, I said instead something quite harmless, like, "Hmmm, how interesting." (This young man was like a reincarnated Steinbeck and Kazantzakis all rolled into one. The plot thickens.)

He went on,

If you've traveled very much, perhaps you've had these same feelings . . . these feelings of running away from something and at the same time running toward something. You can't define it, but you can't shake it out of you either. It's weird. What do I do with this thing that's in there? If I should be running toward it, where do I start?

Now at this point, *I* was the one who was the captive audience. In my wildest imagination I could never have guessed I would one day meet a total stranger who would ask so many of the same questions I too had asked "in my youth." And there he was, right before me. Was I talking with my alter ego? It was weird, indeed, but not for the same reasons he thought.

In my attempt to respond to his universal quandaries I referred to how the soul is always looking for permanence—that it was created for heaven, not earth, and that it "groans" to leave the body and go to that place for which it was created. He listened as I talked. I referred to the Bible, quoting scriptures here and there as I remembered them and as they seemed pertinent. Then he talked about metaphysics, about the incorporeal aspects of the soul.

With that as a springboard for further comments, I told him about Jesus Christ . . . the deliverance he offers from our unregenerate natures, which hold us to this earth and cause us to search continually for peace that only resides in him—a peace he's already provided if we'll accept it. The traveler was very kind, attentive, and interested in all I had to say and asked a few questions, but he told me he just couldn't accept that theology as truth. That he had tried to talk to God, but there was no answer to so many questions he had asked him. "Why doesn't he answer me?" was his closing remark. Then when there was a momentary lull in the conversation, he picked up his backpack, stood to his full height, smiled, thanked me for the "unforgettable" visit, and walked away. I never saw him again.

Who was that person, anyway? I've thought about him a lot since the summer of 1980 on Poros, and not remembering his real name, I have named him "The Voice." In a very real sense, he is the inner voice of every traveler. Whether we know it or not, we are all running away from something as well as running toward something when we travel. We're anticipating that "perfect" trip which will help us discover or rediscover our own souls. We're unconsciously seeking answers to questions we carry around with us all the time. Maybe those answers lie in another culture, in another country, on an island, in the comments or actions of someone we've never met, on a cruise, in a big city, in a tiny village—"anyplace, away from any Here." Isn't that how Steinbeck refers to it?

And there is certainly no question about traveling providing the lift we need. The change does us good. Different people, different scenery. It helps us regroup our forces and resources and it usually causes us to be more content with what we have when we return home.

I've had all those feelings as I have traveled, and most especially when my itinerary has taken me out of this country—far enough away to taste the flavor of another culture. I well remember some of those experiences.

In Germany

I've sat on a tour bus traveling through the ruins of once-beautiful East Berlin, looking at the faces of its imprisoned people walking down the street who gazed back at me out of emptiness or hatred, as I have contemplated the horrors and senselessness of war.

I've walked down the streets of Munich, drinking in the architecture, wondering how the people had the patience for such detailed work, only to find out later that nine million tons of rubble were removed from that city after World War II. I was seeing only what was left.

I've stood in front of Albrecht Dürer's painting, *The Four Apostles*, completed in 1526, which hangs in the Munich Pinakothek Museum, and lost my breath over its beauty and its colors, which are still true. And I've thought about the fact that some things are without price, as our museum guide told us of a wealthy American who offered five million dollars for this painting after the war. The museum turned it down.

In Austria

I've toured the Staatsoper, the famous opera house in Vienna (a beautiful, elegant building), as my well-informed friend and guide related stories about the bombing of that building in

1945; how it was completely destroyed and burned out of control for five days. After the war the townspeople elected to rebuild it first, so they would have a place in which their beloved music could be performed. It took ten years.

I've snapped four of the fastest rolls of film in my life of various views of the snowcovered Alps as my plane was landing in Innsbruck, between them. We were near enough to practically touch those mountains, the majestic handiwork of God.

In Italy

I've spent Easter weekend as one of the house guests of Maestro Nicola Resigno, who lives in a four-hundred-year-old villa on the outskirts of Rome—a building erected during the days of Michelangelo, overlooking a village where he had walked.

I've sung "Clementine" (in my hotel room in Milan) with my friend, Bianca Berini, whom I saw on national television recently as one of the principal singers of the Metropolitan Opera's reproduction of *A Masked Ball*.

I've listened to my dear chorus master, Maestro Mola, who is dead now, play Mozart melodies on a piano in his home. The wall behind him was covered with photographs of his personal friends: Bruno Walter, Richard Strauss, Arturo Toscanini, Gian Carlo Menotti, Pietro Mascagni, Zoltan Kodaly. And I entertained thoughts about spheres of influence: "He knew them, now I know him."

In Argentina

I've had the *best* beef steak I've eaten in my life at a restaurant called "La Estancia" in Buenos Aires, with my father and my older brother and his family, to a background of continuous laughter, jabber, and enjoyment, all to the tune of $27.93. This included steaks for nine people, four salads, four dishes of potatoes, thirteen cold drinks, a bottle of wine, a bottle of mineral water, six sausages, bread, and nine desserts. We still talk about it!

I've waited in the rain to catch a taxi in order to visit the famous Colon Theater. Upon arrival I watched a rehearsal of the ballet *Swan Lake*. Seven of the dancers were acquaintances of mine, with whom I had worked in the Dallas Opera. Small world!

I've stood in a circle of twelve around a table of "high tea" in my brother's home, embracing the persons next to me as Orville led in prayer, first in English, then in Spanish, after which we sang, "Blest Be the Tie That Binds." Within a matter of hours, my father and I were winging our way on a 747 back to North America, and our "trip of a lifetime" (the only time my father ever flew) was behind us.

In Greece

I've gotten lost again and again in the maze of pleasant and inconsequential streets on the island of Mykonos. And I loved every lost moment.

I've stood on the Acropolis and contemplated the meaning and the cost of democracy.

I've disco-danced on the island of Hydra (that "other Camelot") until 5:00 A.M. with a charming Australian journalist who had been invited to Athens by Aristotle Onassis. Then I walked back to my hotel room as the tiny Greek fishing boats were leaving that picturesque harbor in the golden light of dawn. Beautiful!

I've viewed the ruins of Delphi and considered my own youth by comparison.

I've said an emotional goodbye to my "Greek family" on Christmas Day and flown home to America—over eight thousand miles away—with a heart once again filled with unforgettable memories.

I could write an entire book replete with those kinds of statements from my travels. Reflections on the past. Moments of happiness. Questions to ponder. But in each example, there would be the same underlying theme: transition and change.

Everything we do, everything we feel, every place we visit, every treasured moment of enjoyment, every savored second of beauty is temporary. Nothing in this life is permanent. Nothing, except change. Life is not a neat little secure package that is doled out, carefully unwrapped, and completely understood as we eagerly and lovingly accept it. Life is uncertain. It is the teeter-tottering of humanity on a narrow, shaky bridge between the two powers of nature and spirit. Yet, unconsciously perhaps, each of us is searching, with his or her every breath, for that "thing" which will make us happy, will fulfill us and make us feel secure . . . fleeting though it may be in actuality. And truthfully, a great portion of the magnetic appeal of this search is the fact that we know we must capture the moment quickly or it will be gone. "Maybe what I'm looking for is in this next adventure," we say—so we rush to it with open arms. We make our travel plans and we set out. We forget that permanency does not lie on this earth. We forget that the apostle James says:

> Look here, you people who say, "Today or tomorrow we are going to such and such a town, stay there a year, and open up a profitable business." How do you know what is going to happen tomorrow? For the length of your lives is as uncertain as the morning fog—now you see it; soon it is gone.

My travels have only impressed upon me even more that the thing *from* which I am running is myself—that nature which holds me down—and the thing *toward* which I am running is God—that Spirit which lifts me up.

Speaking of that, the biggest trip of my lifetime is coming up. Although the date of departure has not been firmed up, here's the itinerary:

> For the Lord himself will come down from heaven with a mighty shout and with the soul-stirring cry of the archangel and the great trumpet-call of God. And the believers who are dead will be the first to rise to meet the Lord. Then we who are still alive and remain on the earth will be caught up with them in the clouds to meet the Lord in the air and remain with him forever.

That, my fellow travelers, is a liftoff!

Epilogue
THE GOLD

We've come to the close of this document of record, this biography of people and events that have so greatly affected my life. In actuality, they have made it what it is today even though I was unaware of it at the time. That's the way life is oftentimes—we cannot recognize the value of something until we have been away from it for a while, and then looked back upon it in thoughtful retrospection.

Before I write my final sentence in this growth odyssey, however, I want to say a few words about gold. Gold, generally agreed to be one of the first metals known to humanity, is a metallic chemical with certain definable properties. It can be stretched or hammered without breaking because it's not brittle. It can be pressed into various shapes because it's pliable. It is adaptable, amenable, and when yielded to the skilled hand of the metallurgist, it is easily molded into a new form without resisting or returning to its original shape. All of this can be accomplished apart from gold's ever losing its color, lustre, or texture. But because gold is soft and sensitive, it will never be fashioned into a tool or weapon. Its greatest value and beauty is as a pure metal—free from alloys, free from anything that lowers its inherent quality.

Isn't that interesting? When I think of gold, I envision in my mind something that has been refined through a process. I see it as having had extracted from it all the dross and worthless stuff that would cheapen it or cause it to be unattractive.

So too with life. Living is a process. As God, in his wisdom and love, takes us through trials, as he stretches us, presses us into various shapes to refine us and mold us, he does so in order to free us from all the rubbish, the trappings and dross that cause us to lose our significance, individuality, or attractiveness. It is the process of setting us free from ourselves, as well as from anyone or anything that holds us back from what he himself wants to make of us.

This entire book is a cry for freedom. It is heard throughout every page and in every chapter . . . the cry to be free from the things which keep me from being all I am capable of being as a new creature in Christ. This alchemy of my heart has taken fifty years, and it continues. It *will* continue until I am set free of this earth and this body altogether.

Becoming free is not an easy process, nor is it always an enjoyable one. Notwithstanding those facts, there is no greater reason for living. The process is the only thing that gives my life substance and value.

For the last time, then, let's cast a backward glance at the products of this refining process, this alchemy.

First *The Metals:*

> From my grandparents, I learned freedom to be carefree but responsible.
>> —my father, freedom to be tolerant of others.
>> —my mother, freedom to appreciate originality and value creativity.
>> —my older brother, freedom to aim toward excellence.
>> —my younger brother, freedom to overcome the negative.
>> —my friends, freedom to be vulnerable.
>> —my mentors, freedom to revere life and accept death.

Then *The Furnace:*

> From school, I learned freedom from presumption.
>> —opera, freedom from mediocrity.
>> —projects, freedom from impetuosity.

—work, freedom from dissociation.
—solitude, freedom from companionship.
—church, freedom from legalism.
—travels, freedom from permanence.

In *Report to Greco*, Nikos Kazantzakis said that he had "discovered the secret so sought after by medieval alchemists: how to transubstantiate even the basest metal into pure gold." Because, he says,

> the "philosopher's stone" is not something inaccessible and external to man which can be found only by throwing natural laws into confusion; it is our own heart.[1]

Yes. That's where the alchemy takes place—in my heart, in your heart. That's the caldron in which the fire blazes and in which the dross is burnt away. That's the testing place. But the Alchemist who handles *my* heart is Jehovah God, and he knows exactly how hot to make the fire.

1, Nikos Kazantzakis, *Report to Greco* (New York: Bantam Books, 1971), p. 364

Acknowledgements

Without the following seven people, it is doubtful that the book you now hold would ever have found its way between these covers. It would still be either disconnected, random thoughts, floating around in my "heat oppressed brain," or a pile of notebook papers with longhand scribblings. Therefore it gives me great pleasure to express, in print, my particular thanks to these thoughtful individuals.

My Publisher: John Van Diest—the captain of Multnomah Press, who seemed to believe in me when I didn't believe in myself.

My Editors: Julie Cave and Meg Norton—crew members of Multnomah Press whose lovingly critical kindness and experience had the insight and wisdom to delete or reconstruct those things in a manuscript that should never have left my brain in the first place.

My Typist: Nancy King—an unparalleled organizer of facts, fiction, and figures, with the skill and sensitivity to smooth out many a scribbled thought.

My Brother: Orville Swindoll—a man with a mission, who is unbelievably busy, yet with time and thoughtfulness enough to write the foreword to this book.

My Best Friend: Marilyn Meberg—a listener, an encourager, a master of the English language, with a sense of humor that made me laugh when I wanted to cry and lifted me up when the chips were down.

My Greek Comrade: Sophia Stylianidou—who not only introduced me to herself and her uncomplicated, free, sincere way of life, but to the writings of Nikos Kazantzakis, who has helped me learn how to put it into practice.

You seven wonderful people . . . I love you dearly, and I thank you with all my heart. Now, let's celebrate!